PERIPLU

Pocket
THAI
Dictionary

Compiled by
Michael Golding
and
Benjawan Jai-Ua

PERIPLUS

Published by Periplus Editions (HK) Ltd., with editorial offices
at 130 Joo Seng Road, #06-01/03, Singapore 368357

ISBN: 0-7946-0045-X

LCC No: 2003113438

Printed in Singapore

Distributed by:

Asia Pacific
Berkeley Books Pte Ltd
130 Joo Seng Road, 06-01/03
Singapore 368357
Tel: (65) 6280 1330; Fax: (65) 6280 6290
Email: inquiries@periplus.com.sg

Japan
Yaekari Bldg., 3F
5-4-12 Osaki, Shinagawa-ku,
Tokyo 141-0032, Japan
Tel: (03) 5437 0171; Fax: (03) 5437 0755
Email: tuttle-sales@gol.com

North America, Latin America & Europe
Tuttle Publishing
364 Innovation Drive
North Clarendon, VT 05759-9436, USA
Tel: (802) 773 8930; Fax: (802) 773 6993
Email: info@tuttlepublishing.com
www.tuttlepublishing.com

08 07 06 05 04
8 7 6 5 4 3 2 1

Contents

Introduction

This Pocket Dictionary is an indispensable companion for visitors to Thailand and for anyone in the early stages of learning Thai. It contains all the 3,000 or so Thai words that are most commonly encountered in colloquial, everyday speech.

For the sake of clarity, only the most common Thai equivalent(s) for each English word have been given. When an English word has more than one possible meaning, with different Thai equivalents, each meaning is listed separately, accompanied by a clear explanatory gloss. The layout is clear and accessible, with none of the abbreviations and dense nests of entries typical of many small dictionaries.

Pronunciation

You'll no doubt want to dive straight in and get Thai working for you as soon as possible. There are, however, some points to note, the first is that Thai is a tonal language and it has some sounds that might sound strange to a western ear. Hence the purpose of this section is to give you some idea as to how Thai is pronounced and to show you how the tones work. It is a good idea to ask a Thai friend to assist with the pronunciation, especially the tones—you'll notice that each word in this dictionary is given in Thai script together with the imitated pronunciation to aid in your quest to speak Thai.

Romanized Thai

English is a slightly confusing language—individual letters do not correspond to single sounds. Many vowel sounds, for example, can be pronounced using the letter "e," for example "mother," "women," "they," "he," etc. The imitated pronunciation used in this dictionary, on the other hand, is straightforward once you learn the basic rules.

Vowels

Standard five. The "standard" five Thai vowels (*a, e, i, o, u*) are pronounced as in Spanish or Italian:

a (*aa* when long) as in "car"
e (*eh* when long) as in "hey"
i (*ii* when long) as in "free"
o (*oh* when long) as in "go"
u (*uu* when long) as in "true"

These are all pure vowels. Have a Thai friend pronounce the vowels, and take note of *oh* which requires to be said with rounded lips.

New ones. For the four new ones, try to mimic your friend as much as possible. Some of the sounds may be quite funny, so make the most of them.

> *ae* (*aeh* when long) is pronounced as in "fair"
> *aw* as in "fawn"
> *oe* (*oeh* when long) as in "skirt," but feel it under your chin
> *ueh* (*ueh* when long) is said by imagining there's a twig across your mouth and by clenching your teeth while making *euh* noises!

You'll get them easily with practice. Just have a go, and try to closely imitate your friend's pronunciation.

Mixed vowels. There are many vowel combination, which are read as they are spelt.

Consonants

The majority of Thai consonants are like those in English, with a few missing and a couple tossed in. However, the romanized phonetics treat some letters differently to what you may be used to. The *c* is similar to *j*, and *k* is pronounced like a *g* to help it match a pattern. That pattern is given in the following section.

Is there air produced or not? Place your palm in front of your mouth and say "pie" (quite hard and distinctly) and then "by." You should feel a puff of air for the first word. In romanized Thai this is indicated by an *h* after the letter. So

> *ph* as in "pie"
> *th* as in "tie"
> *kh* as in "kite"

all include a puff of air and are called aspirated letters.

Those that do not produce as much air (if any) are

> *b* as in "by"
> *d* as in "die"
> *k* as in "guy"

but not voiced and with the lips pressed together to start.

New-sound consonants. Thai has two new sounds: *p* and *t*, which sound between *ph* and *b*, and between *th* and *d* respectively. To help hear the difference, note that *b* and *d* are voiced—you have to vibrate your vocal cords to say them. The *ph* and *th* are like the English *pas* as in "possible" and *t* as in "terrific." They are certainly not pronounced as in "phone" and "thing!" So, we note that Phuket in the south of Thailand is actually pronounced *phuukèt* (*poohget*)!

The phonetic *p* is produced by starting with the lips slightly pressed together (as some people do to show displeasure), followed by an "explosive" *puu* (rhymes with "zoo"), which means crab.

The *t* is pronounced by starting with the tongue pressed behind the front teeth, then released to say the word. Try *tii* (rhymes with "see") which means to hit.

Practice, practice, practice these new consonants by saying *ph*, *p*, *b* over and over to feel the difference on your lips. Do the same for *th*, *t* and *d*. It helps to give them a vowel like *ii* (as with *tii*), *uu* or better *aw*, as this is the vowel the Thais give them.

Final sounds. Thai final sounds are not released, they are just finished or stopped. For example, say *mat*, but leave your tongue on the roof of your mouth as you get to the *t*. The same for *mak*, *map* and a new ending: *ma* is pronounced by keeping the mouth open after starting. An abrupt ending on a short vowel is called a "glottal stop."

Tones

English has tones, but you may not have noticed them. We use them to extend meaning, but the word itself doesn't change. For example, Mum wants to call James back home after he's run up the street: *céh-ehms*! James arrives, covered in dust: "*cêhms*! Where've you been?." The matter is still about James, but the intonation suggests a different meaning. In Thai, a change in intonation will change the meaning of a word, for example from being pretty *sŭay* to being bad luck *suay*!

Thai has five tones: mid, low, falling, high and rising. After the mid-tone (no mark) these are represented by the symbols ˋ, ˆ, ´ and ˇ. Falling and rising tones are the most important. To say the falling tone, imagine you are throwing your voice off a cliff—it goes up a little, then drops, as in the second "James." To say the rising tone, start low and "sing" the tone upwards—as you might when scolding someone. Ask your Thai friend to show you how and, once again, practice, practice, practice.

Dictionary order

This dictionary follows standard practice for both the Thai script and the romanized Thai. The aspirated consonants *kh*, *ph* and *th* appear within *k*, *p* and *t* respectively. As such, words are easy to look up and are quickly found.

Thai–English

A

aa อา aunt (younger than father)

aacaan อาจารย์ teacher (usually with degree)

aacian อาเจียร to vomit

aachîip อาชีพ occupation, profession

aahǎan อาหาร food

aahǎan chao อาหารเช้า breakfast, morning meal

aahǎan klaang wan อาหารกลางวัน lunch, midday meal

aahǎan thaleh อาหารทะเล seafood

aahǎan yen อาหารเย็น dinner, evening meal

aakàat อากาศ weather, air

aan อาน cart (horsecart)

àan อ่าน to read

àang àap náam อ่างอาบน้ำ bath

àang láang nâa อ่างล้างหน้า wash basin

àap náam อาบน้ำ bathe, take a bath, take a shower

àap náam fàk bua อาบน้ำฝักบัว shower (for washing)

aarom อารมณ์ emotion

àat อาจ may, might

àat (ca) pen pai dâi อาจ(จะ)เป็นไปได้ could well be possible

àat cà, àat ca อาจจะ could, might, may; perhaps, maybe, possibly

aathít thîi lǎeo อาทิตย์ที่แล้ว last week

àatyaakawn อาชญากร criminal

aawút อาวุธ weapon

aayú อายุ age

aayú thâorai อายุเท่าไร how old?

adìit อดีต past, former

ae แอ air (conditioning)

àep แอบ to hide

áeppôen แอ๊ปเปิ้ล apple

ai อาย to be shy, embarrassed

ai ไอ to cough

ai náam ไอน้ำ steam

ailaen ไอร์แลนด์ Ireland

aiskhriim, itiim ไอศครีม ice cream

alài อะไหล่ spare part (of machine)

amehríkaa อเมริกา America

amehríkan อเมริกัน American

amnâat อำนาจ authority (power)

amphoeh อำเภอ Amphoe, district

an อัน *classifier* universal for items of unknown classifier eg. hamburgers, spectacles

angkrìt อังกฤษ British, England

angùn อง่น grapes

antarai อันตราย danger

anúsǎowarii อนุสาวรีย์ monument

anúsǎowarii chaisamǎwráphuum อนุสาวรีย์ชัยสมรภูมิ Victory monument

anúsǎowarii prachaathípàtai อนุสาวรีย์ประชาธิปไตย Democracy monument

anúyâat อนุญาต to let, allow, permit

ao เอา to take

ào อ่าว bay

âo อ้าว sultry, hot; *exclamation*: gracious me!

ao àwk เอาออก to take out, remove

ao cing เอาจริง serious (not funny)

ao maa เอามา to bring

ao pai เอาไป to take (away)

apaatméhn อพาร์ทเมนต์ apartment

arai อะไร what?

arai ìik อะไรอีก anything else?

arai kâw dâi อะไรก็ได้ anything

arai náa อะไรนะ pardon me? what did you say?

A

aràwi อร่อย delicious, tasty

àt thêhp อัดเทป to tape record

àt widiioh อัดวิดีโอ to videotape

athíbai อธิบาย to explain

atraa lâehk plìan อัตราแลกเปลี่ยน rate of exchange for foreign currency

awakàat อวกาศ space (outer)

âwi อ้อย sugarcane

àwk ออก out

àwk càak ออกจาก to leave, depart

àwk pai ออกไป go out, exit

àwk sǐang ออกเสียง to pronounce

âwm อ้อม to detour

àwn อ่อน young

àwn aeh อ่อนแอ weak

âwn wawn อ้อนวอน to plead

àwn yohn อ่อนโยน gentle

áwsàtrehlia ออสเตรเลีย Australia

B

bàa บ่า shoulder

baa บาร์ bar (serving drinks)

bâabâa bàwbàw บ้า ๆ บอ ๆ insane, crazy

bâan บ้าน home, house

bâang บ้าง some

baang บาง thin (of things)

baang hàeng บางแห่ง somewhere

baang kapì บางกะปิ Bangkapi, area north of Sukhumvit Road, 16 km east of Bangkok center

baang kàwk náwi บางกอกน้อย Bangkok Noi, area on west bank 3 1/2 km west of Bangkok center

baang kàwk yài บางกอกใหญ่ Bangkok Yai, area on west bank 3 km SW of Bangkok center

baang khěhn บางเขน Bangkhen, area 3 km south of Don Muang, 17 km NE of Bangkok center

baang khon บางคน somebody, someone

baang khráng baang khrao บางครั้งบางคราว occasionally

baang thii บางที perhaps, probably; sometimes, from time to time

baang yàang บางอย่าง some things

baasàkèhtbawn บาสเก็ตบอล basketball

bàat บาท Thai money, baht

bàat phǎeh บาดแผล wound

bàatthayák บาดทะยัก tetanus

baeh แบ to spread out, unfold

baeh mueh แบมือ to open the hand

baehn แบน flat

bàehp แบบ design, style, kind

bàehp fawm แบบฟอร์ม form

bàeng แบ่ง to divide, share

bai ใบ classifier for containers, leaves and sailing ships

bài บ่าย afternoon (till 4 o'clock)

bai anúyâat ใบอนุญาต license, permit

bai kèp ngoen ใบเก็บเงิน invoice

bai khàp khìi ใบขับขี่ license (for driving)

bai máai ใบไม้ leaf

bai sàng ใบสั่ง order (placed for food, goods); ticket (fine)

bai sàng yaa ใบสั่งยา prescription

bai sèt ใบเสร็จ receipt

bamìi บะหมี่ egg noodles

bancù บรรจุ to load (up)

bandai บันได steps, stairs, ladder

bandai lûean บันไดเลื่อน escalator

bangkaloo บังกะโลว์ lodge, bungalow (guest house)

bangkháp บังคับ force, compel

banphá-burùt บรรพบุรุษ ancestor

banthát บรรทัด ruled line

banthúek บันทึก to note

banthúek khào pracam wan บันทึก ข่าวประจำวัน diary, journal

banyai บรรยาย to lecture, describe

banyaakàat บรรยากาศ climate, atmosphere, ambience

bao เบา light (not heavy)

{"0":0}

bàw náam baadaan บ่อน้ำบาดาล well (for water)

bàwi บ่อย often, frequent

bawrícàak บริจาค to donate

bawríkaan บริการ service

bawrísàt บริษัท company, firm

bawrísùt บริสุทธิ์ pure

bawríwehn บริเวณ vicinity, area

bàwk บอก to tell; let someone know

bàwk khàwp khun บอกขอบคุณ say thank you

bàwk laa บอกลา say goodbye

bàwk sĭa cai บอกเสียใจ say sorry

bawn บอล ball

bàwtaaník kaaden บอตานิค การ์เด้นส์ botanic gardens

bèt เบ็ด fish hook

bia เบียร์ beer

bin บิน to fly

bin บิล bill

bitsakìt บิสกิ๊ต biscuit (salty, cracker)

boeh, mǎi lêhk เบอร์, หมายเลข number

bòehk เบิก to withdraw (money)

bòhk mueh โบกมือ to wave

bohraan โบราณ ancient

bòht โบสถ์ church

bon บน on, at

bòn, ráwng thúk บ่น, ร้องทุกข์ to complain

bòt bàat บทบาท role

bòt khwaam บทความ article (in newspaper)

bòt rian บทเรียน lesson

bòt sŏnthanaa บทสนทนา conversation

bòt sùat mon บทสวดมนต์ prayer

braa บรา bra

bráwkkhawlîi บร็อคคอลี่ broccoli

brèhk เบรค brake

bua บัว lotus

bùak บวก plus

buam บวม swollen

bùea เบื่อ bored

bûeang tôn เบื้องต้น basic

bùkhalík láksanà บุคลิกลักษณะ character (personality)

bun บุญ merit (for the afterlife)

burìi บุหรี่ cigarette

buuchaa บูชา to worship

C

cà, ca จะ shall, will

câa จ้า bright (light), intense, glaring

càak จาก of, from

càak kan จากกัน to separate

caam จาม sneeze

caan จาน dish (particular food), platter, plate

câang จ้าง to hire

càehk แจก hand out

caehkan แจกัน vase

câehng แจ้ง to inform

câehng khwaam แจ้งความ notice

cáekkêt แจ็คเก็ต coat, jacket

cai ใจ heart, mind

cài จ่าย to pay

cai dii ใจดี kind, good (of persons)

cai kwâang ใจกว้าง generous

cài láeo จ่ายแล้ว paid

cam จำ to remember

cam dâi จำได้ to recognize

camnuan จำนวน amount

campen จำเป็น necessary, to need

camùuk จมูก nose

cang จัง very (intensifies)

cangwàt จังหวัด province

câo bàao เจ้าบ่าว bridegroom

câo mâeh เจ้าแม่ goddess

câo nâa thîi เจ้าหน้าที่ official, formal; authority (person in charge); staff

câo nâa thîi tamrùat เจ้าหน้าที่ตำรวจ police officer

câo phâap เจ้าภาพ host

câo sǎo เจ้าสาว bride

càp จับ to capture, catch, grab

càt จัด to arrange; extreme, intense

THAI–ENGLISH

C

càt hâi dii khûen จัดให้เรียบร้อย to tidy up

càt hâi mii... จัดให้มี ... to make available

càt kaan จัดการ manage, succeed, organize, sort out, deal with

càt tó จัดโต๊ะ lay the table

catùrát จตุรัส square, town square

caw phâap จอภาพ screen (of computer)

cawng จอง to reserve (seats, tickets)

càwt rót จอดรถ to park a vehicle

cèp เจ็บ sore, hurt (injured)

cèp mâak เจ็บมาก painful

cèt เจ็ด seven

cèt sìp เจ็ดสิบ seventy

chá cháa ช้าๆ slowly

cháa ช้า slow

chaa ชา tea; numb

chaam ชาม bowl

cháang ช้าง elephant

châang ช่าง tradesperson

châang f ĭimueh ช่างฝีมือ craftsperson, tradesperson

châang tàt phŏm ช่างตัดผม barber

châat ชาติ nation, country

chabàp ฉบับ *classifier* for newspapers and documents

châeh khăeng แช่แข็ง to freeze, frozen

chaehmpîan แชมเปี้ยน champion

chai ชาย male

chái ใช้ to use, utilize

châi ใช่ yes

chăi ฉาย to shine a light

chai daehn ชายแดน border (between countries)

chái dâi ใช้ได้ valid

chai hàat ชายหาด beach

chai yoh ไชโย cheers!

chák ชัก to persuade; to have convulsions

chalăam ฉลาม shark

chalàat ฉลาด smart, intelligent

chalăwng ฉลอง to celebrate

chalìa เฉลี่ย average (numbers)

chám ช้ำ bruised

chamnaan ชำนาญ expert

chamrút, sĭa hăi ชำรุด, เสียหาย damage

chán ฉัน I, me

chán ชั้น layer, level, story (of a building); class, category

chaná ชนะ to win

chaná, tham hâi pháeh ชนะ, ทำให้แพ้ beat (to defeat)

châng ชั่ง to weigh

chanít ชนิด type, sort

chanít năi, bàehp năi ชนิดไหน, แบบไหน what kind of?

châo เช่า to hire, rent

cháo เช้า morning

chao airít / airís ชาวไอริช Irish

chao bâan ชาวบ้าน villager

chao indohnisia ชาวอินโดนิเซีย Indonesian

chao khamĕhn ชาวเขมร Cambodian

chao khăo, phào ชาวเขา, เผ่า tribe

chao maalehsia ชาวมาเลเซีย Malaysian

cháo mûeht เช้ามืด dusk

chao phamâa ชาวพม่า Burmese

chao phúehn mueang ชาวพื้นเมือง indigenous

chao phút ชาวพุทธ Buddhist

chao sakàwt ชาวสก็อต Scottish, Scots

chao tàang prathêht ชาวต่างประเทศ foreigner

chao tawan tòk ชาวตะวันตก westerner

cháo trùu เช้าตรู่ dawn, very early

chao wehl(s) ชาวเวลซ์ Welsh

chao wîatnaam ชาวเวียดนาม Vietnamese

chao yîipùn ชาวญี่ปุ่น Japanese

chapháw เฉพาะ only, exclusively for

chát cehn ชัดเจน distinct, very clear
cháwn ช้อน spoon
cháwp ชอบ to be fond of; like, be pleased by
cháwp mâak kwàa ชอบมากกว่า to prefer
cháwkkhohláet ช็อคโคแล็ต chocolate
châwng khâehp ช่องแคบ strait, narrow channel
châwng khlâwt ช่องคลอด vagina
châwng tháwng ช่องท้อง abdomen
chên เช่น for example
chên nán เช่นนั้น such
chét เช็ด to wipe
chǐao chaan เชี่ยวชาญ to be skilled, expert
chíi ชี้ point out
chìi pàtsawá ฉี่, ปัสสาวะ to urinate
chìik ฉีก to tear, rip
chìit ฉีด to inject
chìit sapreh ฉีดสเปรย์ to spray
chìit wáksiin ฉีดวัคซีน vaccination
chiiwít ชีวิต life
chim ชิม to taste (sample)
chín ชิ้น piece, item, bit (part), classifier for parts
choehn เชิญ to invite (formally); please (go ahead)
chóeht เช็ด shirt with collar
chǒei เฉย still, impartial, indifferent
chôhk โชค luck
chôhk dii โชคดี lucky, good luck!
chôhk dii thîi... โชคดีที่... fortunately
chôhk rái โชคร้าย unluck(il)y, unfortunately
chom ชม to admire
chom wiu ชมวิว to view, look at
chomphuu ชมพู pink
chomphûu ชมพู่ rose apple
chon ชน to collide
chon klùm náwi ชนกลุ่มน้อย ethnic group

chonabòt ชนบท country (rural area)
chûa khanà ชั่วขณะ moment (instant)
chûa khrao ชั่วคราว temporary
chûai ช่วย to assist, help; please (request for help)
chûai dûai ช่วยด้วย help!
chûai lǔea ช่วยเหลือ to rescue
chûamohng ชั่วโมง hour, classifier for hours
chuan ชวน to invite (ask along)
chûea เชื่อ to believe
chûea fang เชื่อฟัง to obey
chúea raa เชื้อรา fungus
chûeak เชือก rope, string
chûeang เชื่อง tame
chûeh ชื่อ called, named, given name
chûeh nǎng ชื่อหนัง title (of book, film)
chúehn ชื้น damp, humid
chùk chǒehn ฉุกเฉิน emergency
chǔn, phèt ฉุน, เผ็ด spicy
chúp ชุบ to soak
chút ชุด set
chút chán nay ชุดชั้นใน underwear
chút nawn ชุดนอน nightclothes, pajamas
chút ráp khàehk ชุดรับแขก loungeroom furniture
chút sûea phâa ชุดเสื้อผ้า dress, frock
chút wâi náam ชุดว่ายน้ำ swimming costume, swimsuit
ciin จีน China, Chinese
ciin klaang จีนกลาง "central China," Mandarin
cing จริง true
cing cing จริง ๆ really, truly, indeed!
cing lǒeh จริงหรือ really?
cîngcòk จิ้งจก house lizard
cingcôo จิงโจ้ kangaroo
cîngrìit จิ้งหรีด cricket (insect)
coeh เจอ to meet, find
coeh caang เจือจาง thin (of liquids)
cohm tii โจมตี to attack (in war)

com จม to sink

com náam จมน้ำ to drown

con จน poor

con krathâng จนกระทั่ง until

còp จบ to end (finish)

còt nóht จดโน้ต to note down

còtmǎi จดหมาย letter; post, mail

còtmǎi long thabian จดหมายลงทะเบียน registered post

cuan จวน approaching, almost

cùeht จืด bland

cueng จึง consequently, therefore

cùt จุด point, dot

cùt cùt จุดๆ spotted (pattern)

cùt fai จุดไฟ to light a fire

cùt mǎi plai thaang จุดหมายปลายทาง destination

cùt mûngmǎi จุดมุ่งหมาย purpose

cùt rôehm tôn จุดเริ่มต้น origin

cùup จูบ kiss

D

dàa wâa ด่าว่า attack (with words)

daaraa ดารา movie/TV star

daehng แดง red

dàeht แดด sunshine

dàeht àwk แดดออก sunny

dâi ด้าย thread

dâi, dâi ได้ to be able to, can; get to, gain

dâi ráp ได้รับ get, receive

dâi ráp anúyâat ได้รับอนุญาต to be allowed to

dâi ráp bàat cèp ได้รับบาดเจ็บ to be injured

dâi-yin ได้ยิน to hear

dam ดำ black

dang ดัง famous, loud (sound)

dâng doehm ดั้งเดิม traditional

dang nán ดังนั้น so, therefore

dang tàw pai níi ดังต่อไปนี้ following

dao เดา to guess

dao ดาว star

dàp ดับ go out (fire, candle)

dàt phǒm ดัดผม to perm hair

dàwk bîa ดอกเบี้ย interest (money)

dàwk bua ดอกบัว lotus flower

dàwk kalàm ดอกกะหล่ำ cauliflower

dàwk mái ดอกไม้ flower

dáwktôeh ด็อกเตอร์ Doctor (Ph.D.)

dawn ดอล dollar (colloq.)

dawng ดอง cured, preserved (fruit)

dèk เด็ก child (young person)

dèk chai เด็กชาย boy

dèk nákrian เด็กนักเรียน schoolchild

dèk phûu yǐng เด็กผู้หญิง girl

dètkhàat เด็ดขาด absolutely

diao เดียว single, one, one and the same

dǐao เดี่ยว in a moment, just a moment

dǐao níi เดี๋ยวนี้ right now, now

dǐao níi ehng เดี๋ยวนี้เอง just now

dichán ดิฉัน I (female speaking)

dii ดี fine (okay), good, nice, well

dii cai ดีใจ glad

dii khûen ดีขึ้น better, get (improve)

dii kwàa ดีกว่า better

dii mâak ดีมาก well done!

dii thîi sùt ดีที่สุด best

dii wii dii ดีวีดี DVD

diipháatmén satoh ดิพาร์ตเมนท์สโตร์ department store

din ดิน earth, soil, ground

dinsǎw ดินสอ pencil

dìp ดิบ raw, uncooked, rare

doehm เดิม former, previous

doehn เดิน to walk

doehn maa, doehn pai เดินมา, เดินไป on foot (coming, going)

doehn pai dâi เดินไปได้ walking distance

doehn thaang เดินทาง to travel

doehn thaang doi plàwt phai ná เดินทางโดยปลอดภัยนะ bon voyage!

dohn โดน passive form (acted on by ...)

doi โดย by (author, artist); by way of, by means of
doi bang-oehn โดยบังเอิญ accidentally, by chance
doi chapháw โดยเฉพาะ particularly, especially
doi mâi mii โดยไม่มี without
doi mâi tângcai โดยไม่ตั้งใจ by chance
doi pòkkatì โดยปกติ normally
doi rótfai โดยรถไฟ rail: by rail
doi sîn choehng โดยสิ้นเชิง complete (thorough)
doi thûa pai โดยทั่วไป generally
doisǎan โดยสาร travel, take passage
dòk ดก abundant, plentiful
dom ดม to smell
dontrii ดนตรี music
dù ดุ fierce
dù ดุ fierce, cross
dù rái ดุร้าย cruel
dûai ด้วย as well, too, also
dûai kan ด้วยกัน together
dûai khwaam praathanǎa dii ด้วยความปรารถนาดี best wishes
dûai khwaam sǐa cai ด้วยความเสียใจ regrettably
dûai khwaam wǎng ด้วยความหวัง hopefully
dûai khwaam yindii ด้วยความยินดี with pleasure
dûai wíthii ด้วยวิธี ... by means of, using the method of
dùan ด่วน urgent, express
duang can ดวงจันทร์ moon
duean เดือน month
dùeat เดือด boiling
dûeh ดื้อ determined, stubborn
dùehm ดื่ม to drink
dùek ดึก late at night
dueng ดึง to pull
dueng ao wái ดึงเอาไว้ to restrain

dusìt ดุสิต Dusit, area 5 km NE from Bangkok center
duu ดู to look at, see, to watch (show, movie)
duu laeh ดูแล to take care of
duu mǔean ดูเหมือน to seem
duu mǔeankan ดูเหมือนกัน to look alike
duu sí ดูซิ look!
duu thâa thaang ดูท่าทาง look, seem, appear
duu thùuk ดูถูก to insult, look down on someone
dùut ดูด to suck

E

èhkasǎan เอกสาร document, letter
ehng เอง self
ehsia เอเชีย Asia
en เอ็น tendon

F

fǎa ฝา lid
fàa ฝ่า to go against, violate
fáa ฟ้า sky
fáa phàa ฟ้าผ่า lightning
fǎa phanǎng ฝาผนัง wall (of a room or building)
fáa ráwng ฟ้าร้อง thunder
fàak ฝาก leave behind for safekeeping
faehn แฟน fan (admirer), boy/girlfriend
faehnsìi แฟนซี fancy
fáek(s) แฟกซ์ fax (message or machine)
fai ไฟ fire; light (lamp); electricity
fâi ฝ้าย cotton
fai chǎi ไฟฉาย flashlight, torch
fai cháek ไฟแช็ค lighter
fai fáa ไฟฟ้า electric, electricity
fai mâi ไฟไหม้ on fire

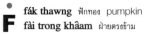

F

fák thawng ฟักทอง pumpkin

fài trong khâam ฝ่ายตรงข้าม opponent

fan ฟัน tooth, teeth

fǎn ฝัน to dream

fǎn klaang wan ฝันกลางวัน to daydream

fang ฟัง to listen, listen to

fàng ฝั่ง bank (river)

fang yùu ฟังอยู่ listening

fâo เฝ้า watch over, guard

fâo yaam เฝ้ายาม to guard

faràng ฝรั่ง caucasian, westerner; guava fruit

faràngsèht ฝรั่งเศส France, French

fàw ฝ่อ to wither, wilt

fawng náam ฟองน้ำ sponge

fiim ฟิล์ม film (camera)

filíppin ฟิลิปปินส์ Philippines

flàet แฟล็ต flat, apartment

foehnítcoeh เฟอร์นิเจอร์ furniture

fǒn ฝน showers, rain

fǒn tòk ฝนตก to rain

fùek hàt ฝึกหัด to practice

fùn ฝุ่น dirt, filth, dust

fút ฟุต foot (length)

fút bawn ฟุตบอล soccer

H

há ฮะ familiar polite particle (male for **khráp**, female for **khá**)

hâa ห้า five

hǎa หา to look for, look up (find in book), search for

hǎa maa dâi หามาได้ to earn

hâa sìp ห้าสิบ fifty

hǎa yâak หายาก rare (scarce)

hâaddís ฮาร์ดดิสก์ hard disk

hâam ห้าม forbidden to ...

hâam ห้าม to forbid

hàan ห่าน goose

hǎan dûai หารด้วย divided by

hàang ห่าง far apart from

hǎang หาง tail

hâang sapphasínkháa ห้างสรรพสินค้า department store

hàat หาด beach

haehm แฮม ham

hâehng แห้ง dry

hâehng láehng แห้งแล้ง dry (weather), drought

hàeng แห่ง of; classifier for places

hàeng châat แห่งชาติ national

hâi ให้ to give; to, for; to allow, have something done

hǎi หาย lost, missing

hâi aahǎan ให้อาหาร to feed

hâi aphai ให้อภัย to forgive

hǎi cai หายใจ to breathe

hâi châo ให้เช่า to rent out

hâi kaan ให้การ to plead (in court)

hâi khuehn ให้คืน to return, give back

hǎi pai, mâi yùu หายไป, ไม่อยู่ absent

hǎi wai wai หายไวๆ get well soon!

hâi yuehm ให้ยืม to lend

hàk หัก broken, snapped (of bones, etc.)

hal-lǒh ฮัลโหล hello! (on phone)

hàn หั่น cut, slice

hǎn หัน to turn towards

hǎn phuangmaalai หันพวงมาลัย to steer

hǎo หาว yawn

hàw เห่า to bark

hàw ห่อ to parcel, wrap

hǎw khawi หอคอย tower

hàw khǎwng ห่อของ package

hǎw phák หอพัก lodgings, dormitory

hǎwi หอย shellfish

hǎwi naang rom หอยนางรม oyster

hǎwi thâak หอยทาก snail

hǎwm หอม sweet smelling, fragrant

hǎwm yài หอมใหญ่ onion

hâwng ห้อง room (in house, hotel)

hâwng kong ฮ่องกง Hong Kong

K

hâwng náam ห้องน้ำ restroom, toilet (bathroom)

hâwng nawn ห้องนอน bedroom

hâwng phák ห้องพัก restroom (for rest)

hâwng samùt ห้องสมุด library

hâwng thŏhng ห้องโถง hall

hèht kaan เหตุการณ์ happening, incident, event

hèht phŏn เหตุผล reason

hĕn เห็น to see

hĕn dûai เห็นด้วย to agree

hĕn kàeh tua เห็นแก่ตัว mean (cruel)

hĕn pen phayaan เห็นเป็นพยาน to witness

hèt เห็ด mushrooms

hĭi หี vagina (colloq.)

hìip หีบ chest (box)

himá หิมะ snow

himá tòk หิมะตก to snow

hĭn หิน rock, stone

hĭn pàkaarang หินปะการัง coral

hĭu หิ้ว to carry

hĭu หิว to be hungry

hĭu náam หิวน้ำ to be thirsty

hòk หก six

hòk หก spill (liquid)

hòk lóm หกล้ม to fall over

hòk sìp หกสิบ sixty

hòt หด to shrink

hŭa หัว head

hŭa cai หัวใจ heart

hŭa hăwm หัวหอม onion

hŭa khâw หัวข้อ topic

hŭa láan หัวล้าน bald

hŭaráw หัวเราะ to laugh

hŭaráw yáw หัวเราะเยาะ to laugh at

hûn sùan หุ้นส่วน partner (in business)

hŭng หุง cook (rice)

hùp khăo หุบเขา valley

hùp pàak หุบปาก close the mouth, shut up, be speechless

hŭu หู ear

hŭu nùak หูหนวก deaf

I

ìik ...อีก again

ìik อีก ... another (different); else, more

ìik an nùeng อีกอันหนึ่ง another one

ìik yàang nueng อีกอย่างหนึ่ง by the way, another thing

iimeh(l) อีเมล์ email (message)

ilék thrawník อิเล็กทรอนิค electronic

ìm อิ่ม to be full, eaten one's fill

indohnisia อินโดนิเซีย Indonesia

intoehnét อินเตอร์เน็ต Internet

ìtaalii อิตาลี Italy, Italian

ìtchăa อิจฉา envy, jealous

ìtsalaam, ìslaam อิสลาม Islam

ìtsarà อิสระ free, independent

ìtsaràphâap อิสรภาพ freedom

itthíphon อิทธิพล influence

K

kaafaeh กาแฟ coffee

kaan... การ... the action of...

kaan ai การไอ cough

kaan bàat cèp การบาดเจ็บ injury

kaan càak pai การจากไป departure

kaan caraacawn การจราจร traffic

kaan càt andàp การจัดอันดับ ranking

kaan càtkaan, kaan waang phăehn การจัดการ, การวางแผน arrangements, planning

kaan cawng การจอง reservation

kaan chìit การฉีด injection

kaan chon การชน collision

kaan doehn thaang การเดินทาง trip, journey

kaan duu thùuk การดูถูก insult

kaan fĭimueh การฝีมือ handicraft

kaan fùek การฝึก training

kaan fùek hàt การฝึกหัด practice

kaan hâi aphai การให้อภัย forgiveness, mercy

K

kaan kàe salàk การแกะสลัก carving

kaan kàw sâang การก่อสร้าง building, construction

kaan khàeng khǎn การแข่งขัน competition

kaan khamùat khíu การขมวดคิ้ว frown

kaan khào การข่าว press, journalism

kaan kratham การกระทำ action

kaan lót การลด reduction

kaan lûeak tâng การเลือกตั้ง election

kaan maa thǔeng การมาถึง arrival

kaan mueang การเมือง politics

kaan nam khâo การนำเข้า import

kaan patìbàt ngaan การปฏิบัติงาน performance

kaan patìsèht การปฏิเสธ refusal

kaan phanan การพนัน gamble

kaan phǎo mâi การเผาไหม้ burn (injury)

kaan phátanaa การพัฒนา development

kaan phluu กานพลู cloves

kaan phôehm khûen การเพิ่มขึ้น increase

kaan rópkuan การรบกวน bother, disturbance

kaan sadaehng การแสดง display

kaan sàwp การสอบ exam, test

kaan sǐa salà การเสียสละ sacrifice

kaan sòng àwk การส่งออก export

kaan sùeksǎa การศึกษา education

kaan tàehng, kaan khǐan การแต่ง, การเขียน composition, writings

kaan tàtsǐn cai การตัดสินใจ decision

kaan tàwp sanǎwng การตอบสนอง reaction, response

kaan tên ram การเต้นรำ dance

kaan thák thai การทักทาย greetings

kaan tham aahǎan การทำอาหาร cooking, cuisine

kaan thaw การทอ weaving

kaan thòk panhǎa การถกปัญหา discussion

kaan thon thúk การทนทุกข์ suffering

kaan tìt tàw การติดต่อ contact, connection

kaan wát การวัด measurement

kaangkehng กางเกง trousers, pants

kaangkehng khǎa sân กางเกงขาสั้น shorts (short trousers)

kaangkehng nai กางเกงใน underpants, panties

kaatuun การ์ตูน cartoon

kàe แกะ sheep

kàe salàk แกะสลัก to carve

kaeh แก he, she, they (informal)

kàeh แก่ old (of persons)

kâeh แก้ to fix (repair)

kâeh hâi thùuk แก้ให้ถูก to correct

kàeh kwàa แก่กว่า older, elder

kâeh panhǎa แก้ปัญหา to solve (a problem)

kâeh phâa แก้ผ้า to get undressed

kâeh tàang แก้ต่าง to defend (with words)

kâehm แก้ม cheek

kaehng แกง curry

kâeo แก้ว glass (for drinking)

kài ไก่ chicken, poultry

kalàm dàwk กล่ำดอก cauliflower

kalàm plii กล่ำปลี cabbage

kam mueh กำมือ clench the fist

kamcàt กำจัด to rid, get rid of

kamlang กำลัง to be presently doing; strength, power, (armed) force

kamlang doehn thaang กำลังเดินทาง on the way

kamnòt กำหนด program, schedule

kamphaehng กำแพง wall (of a yard or town)

kamphaehng praasàat กำแพงปราสาท fortress wall

kamrai กำไร profit

kan กัน together, mutually; to prevent

kan thòe กันเถอะ let's (suggestion)

K

kankrai กรรไกร scissors
kanyaayon กันยายน September
kao กาว glue
kao เกา to scratch lightly
kào เก่า old (of things)
kâo ก้าว step
kâo เก้า nine
kâo nâa ก้าวหน้า advance, go forward
kâo sìp เก้าสิบ ninety
kâo-îi เก้าอี้ chair
kâo-îi tháo khǎehn เก้าอี้เท้าแขน armchair
kaolǐi nǔea เกาหลีเหนือ Korea, North
kaolǐi tâi เกาหลีใต้ Korea, South
kàp กับ with, and
kàp khâo กับข้าว dishes with rice
kapì กะปิ fish paste
karákadaakhom กรกฎาคม July
karunaa กรุณา please ... (formal)
kasèht เกษตร agriculture
kàt กัด to bite
kàw เกาะ island
kâw ก็ also, well ...
kàw tâng ก่อตั้ง to establish, set up
káwf กอล์ฟ golf
kàwn ก่อน first, earlier, before
kâwn ก้อน classifier for lump-like objects
kàwn lûang nâa ก่อนล่วงหน้า beforehand, earlier
kàwn níi ก่อนนี้ earlier, before this
kawng tháp กองทัพ troops, armed force(s)
kàwt กอด to embrace, hug
kéh เก๊ fake
kěh เก๋ with it, stylish, chic
kehm เกม match, game
kèng เก่ง clever, smart, good at something
kèp เก็บ to save, collect, keep
kèp khǎwng เก็บของ to pack (luggage)
kèp khûen เก็บขึ้น pick up, lift (something)

kèp tó เก็บโต๊ะ clear away the table
khá คะ female polite particle (questioning)
khâ ค่ะ female polite particle (stating)
khàa ข่า galanga
khâa ค่า value (cost)
khâa ฆ่า kill, murder
khǎa ขา leg
khǎa àwn ขาอ่อน thigh
khâa câang ค่าจ้าง wages
khâa chái cài ค่าใช้จ่าย cost, expenses
khâa doisǎan ค่าโดยสาร fare
khâa pràp ค่าปรับ fine (punishment)
khâa râatchakaan ข้าราชการ officials (government)
khâa râatchakaan ข้าราชการ public servant
khâa thammaniam ค่าธรรมเนียม fee
khâam ข้าม across, cross, go over
khâam fàak ข้ามฝาก to cross the river
kháan ค้าน opposed, in opposition
khaang คาง chin
khâang ข้าง side
kháang khuehn ค้างคืน to stay overnight
khàat ขาด lacking
khàat mòt ขาดหมด worn out (clothes)
khàat pai ขาดไป missing (absent)
khàat thun ขาดทุน to lose profit
khâat wâa... คาดว่า... to expect...
khàehk แขก guest
khàehk phûu mii kìat แขกผู้มีเกียรติ guest of honour
khǎehn แขน arm
khaehnadaa แคนาดา Canada
khâehp แคบ narrow
khaehràwt แครอท carrot
khàeng แข่ง to compete
khǎeng แข็ง to be hard (solid), stiff, firm

khǎeng raehng แข็งแรง strong

khài ไข่ egg

khài ไข้ fever

khǎi ขาย for sale, to sell

khài ciao ไข่เจียว omelette

khài dao ไข่ดาว eggs sunny side up

khǎi man ไขมัน fat, grease

khǎi mòt láeo ขายหมดแล้ว sold out

khài múk ไข่มุก pearl

khài múk thiam ไข่มุกเทียม cultured pearl

khǎi láeo ขายแล้ว sold

khài lûak ไข่ลวก soft boiled egg

khài tôm ไข่ต้ม hard boiled egg

khâi wàt yài ไข้หวัดใหญ่ flu

khài yîao máa ไข่เยี่ยวม้า black preserved egg

kham คำ word

khǎm ขำ to be funny, amusing, witty

kham choehn คำเชิญ invitation

kham náenam คำแนะนำ advice, suggestion, instruction, direction

kham nam nâa chûeh คำนำหน้าชื่อ title (of person)

kham praasǎi คำปราศรัย speech

kham ráwng thúk คำร้องทุกข์ complaint

kham sàng คำสั่ง command, order

kham sàp คำศัพท์ vocabulary

kham tàwp คำตอบ answer, response

kham thǎam คำถาม question

kham tuean คำเตือน warning

kham yók yâwng คำยกย่อง praise

khamǒehn เขมร Cambodia

khamnuan คำนวณ to calculate

khamoi ขโมย to steal, a thief, thieves

khamùat khíu ขมวดคิ้ว to frown

khamùk khamǔa ขมุกขมัว dull (weather)

khan คัน to itch; *classifier* for vehicles, umbrellas, spoons and forks

khân ขั้น increment, step

khanà níi ขณะนี้ at the present moment

khanà thîi ขณะที่ meanwhile, while

khanàat ขนาด size

khâng bon ข้างบน upstairs

khâng khâang ข้าง ๆ beside

khâng lâang ข้างล่าง below, downstairs

khâng lǎng ข้างหลัง rear, tail, behind

khâng nâa ข้างหน้า before (in front of), front

khâng nai ข้างใน inside of, inside

khâng nâwk ข้างนอก outside of, outside

khâng tâi ข้างใต้ bottom (base)

khanǒm ขนม pastry, sweets, dessert

khanǒm khéhk ขนมเค้ก cake

khanǒm pang ขนมปัง bread

khanǒm wǎan ขนมหวาน confectionery

khanǒm, lûuk om ขนม, ลูกอม sweets, candy

khanǒmpang kràwp ขนมปังกรอบ cracker, salty biscuit

khanǔn ขนุน jackfruit

khào เข่า knee

khào ข่าว news

khâo ข้าว rice (plant)

khâo เข้า to enter

khǎo เขา she, her, he, him, they, them

khǎo ขาว white

khǎo เขา mountain

khâocai เข้าใจ understand

khâocai phìt เข้าใจผิด to misunderstand

khâo hǎa เข้าหา to approach (in space)

khâo khiu เข้าคิว to queue, line up

khâo lǎam ข้าวหลาม glutinous rice with coconut milk roasted in bamboo

K

khâo maa เข้ามา come in

khâo nĭao ข้าวเหนียว sticky, glutinous rice

khâo phôht ข้าวโพด sweetcorn

khâo phôht ข้าวโพด corn, grain

khâo rûam เข้าร่วม to join in together, attend

khâo săalii ข้าวสาลี wheat

khâo săan ข้าวสาร rice (uncooked grains)

khâo sŭai ข้าวสวย rice (cooked)

kháotôeh เคาน์เตอร์ counter (for paying, buying tickets)

khàp ขับ to drive a vehicle

kháp คับ to be tight (not loose)

khát kháan คัดค้าน to protest, object

khàt ngao ขัดเงา to polish

khaw คอ neck

khâw ข้อ body joint

kháw เคาะ to knock

khăw ขอ to ask for, request (informally), apply for permission, please

khâw bòk phrâwng ข้อบกพร่อง defect

khaw hăwi คอหอย throat

khâw khwaam ข้อความ message

khâw mueh ข้อมือ wrist

khăw ráwng ขอร้อง to request (formally)

khăw sadaehng khwaam yindii dûai ขอแสดงความยินดีด้วย congratulations!

khăw sanŏeh ข้อเสนอ offering

khaw săw ค.ศ. anno domini, CE

khâw sàwk ข้อศอก elbow

khăw thaang nàwi ขอทางหน่อย excuse me! (getting past)

khâw tháo ข้อเท้า ankle

khâw thét cing ข้อเท็จจริง fact

khăw thôht ขอโทษ to apologize, sorry!, excuse me!

khâw tòklong ข้อตกลง agreement

khăw yuehm ขอยืม to borrow

khawi คอย to wait for

khâwi ค่อย gradually, little by little

khâwi yang chûa ค่อยยังชั่ว better, get (be cured)

khawmphiwtôeh คอมพิวเตอร์ computer

khâwmuun ข้อมูล information

kháwn ค้อน hammer

khâwn khâang ค่อนข้าง rather, fairly

khăwng ของ thing(s), belongings; belongs to, (see also **khăwng**)

khăwng ของ belongs to, possessive "of"

khăwng chán ของฉัน my, mine

khăwng hăi ของหาย lost property

khăwng kào ของเก่า antiques

khăwng khăo ของเขา his, hers, their, theirs

khăwng khwăn ของขวัญ present (gift)

khăwng lên ของเล่น toy

khăwng rao ของเรา our

khăwng sùan tua ของส่วนตัว own, personal

khăwng thiam ของเทียม imitation items

khăwng thîi ralúek ของที่ระลึก souvenir

khăwng wăan ของหวาน sweet, dessert

khàwp ขอบ border, edge

khàwp khun ขอบคุณ to thank, thank you

khayà ขยะ garbage, rubbish

khayăi ขยาย to expand, grow larger

khayăn ขยัน hardworking, diligent

khayào เขย่า to shake something

khem เค็ม to taste salty

khĕm เข็ม needle

khĕm khàt เข็มขัด belt

khêm khôn เข้มข้น to concentrate (liquid)

khîan เคี่ยน to whip, beat

khĭan เขียน to write

K

khĭan còtmăi เขียนจดหมาย to correspond (write letters)

khĭan nóht เขียนโน้ต note (written)

khĭan tàwp เขียนตอบ to reply (in writing)

khĭang เขียง chopping board

khíao เคี้ยว to chew

khĭao เขียว green

khìi ขี่ to ride

khîi ขี้ shit, to shit

khîi ai ขี้อาย given to shyness

khîi kìat ขี้เกียจ lazy

khîi mao ขี้เมา given to be intoxicated

khîi nĭao ขี้เหนียว stingy

khîi phûeng ขี้ผึ้ง wax

khiibàwd คีย์บอร์ด keyboard (of computer)

khiim คีม pliers

khĭng ขิง ginger

khít คิด to think, to have an opinion

khít thŭeng คิดถึง to miss (as a loved one)

khiu คิว queue, line

khíu คิ้ว eyebrow

khlái คล้าย similar

khlawng คลอง canal, k(h)long

khlâwng คล่อง fluent

khlawng càn คลองจั่น Khlongcan, area 11 km ENE of Bangkok

khlawng săan คลองสาน Khlongsan, area 2^1/$_2$ km south of Bangkok center

khlawng tan คลองตัน Khlongtan, on railway line 11 km east of Bangkok

khlawng toei คลองเตย Khlongtoey, port 8 km SE of Bangkok

khlâwt lûuk คลอดลูก to give birth

khlûean thîi เคลื่อนที่ to move

khlûehn คลื่น wave (in sea)

khlùi ขลุ่ย flute

khlum คลุม to cover

khlum khruea คลุมเครือ to be vague

khohm โคม lamp

khóhng โค้ง curved, convex

khoei เคย used to ..., have ever ...

khŏei เขย male in-law

khoei pai เคยไป have been somewhere

khoei tham เคยทำ have done something

khom คม sharp

khŏm ขม bitter

khon คน person, people, *classifier for people*

khôn ข้น thick (of liquids)

khŏn ขน body hair

khon amehríkan คนอเมริกัน American (person)

khon áwsàtrehlia คนออสเตรเลีย Australian (person)

khon chái คนใช้ servant

khon ciin คนจีน Chinese (person)

khon diao คนเดียว on one's own, alone, single (only one), sole

khon fâw ráan, khon khăi คนเฝ้าร้าน, คนขาย shopkeeper

khon kawlĭi คนเกาหลี Korean

khon khâi คนไข้ patient (doctor's)

khon khàp คนขับ driver

khon kohng, khon khîi kohng คนโกง, คนขี้โกง cheat, someone who cheats

khon lao คนลาว Laotian

khón phóp ค้นพบ to discover

khon plàehk nâa คนแปลกหน้า stranger

khŏn sàt ขนสัตว์ wool

khon sòehp คนเสิร์ฟ waiter, waitress

khon tham aahăan คนทำอาหาร cook (person)

khon thîi... คนที่... one who, the one which

khong คง probably, surely

khòp khăn ขบขัน humorous

khrai ใคร who?

khrai kâw dâi ใครก็ได้ anybody, anyone

khráng ครั้ง *classifier* for times, occasions

khrao เครา beard

khráp ครับ *male polite particle* (questioning or stating)

khráw rái เคราะห์ร้าย misfortune

khrâwp khrawng ครอบครอง to overcome

khrâwp khrua ครอบครัว family

khrêng khrát เคร่งครัด strict

khriim ครีม cream

khrístian, chao khrít คริสเตียน, ชาวคริสต์ Christian

khrohng โครง frame

khrohng sâang โครงสร้าง structure

khrók ครก mortar (for grinding foods)

khróp thûan ครบถ้วน complete, altogether

khrù khrà ขรุขระ rough, uneven

khrua ครัว kitchen

khruea khài เครือข่าย network

khrûeang ครึ่ง half

khrûeang เครื่อง machine

khrûeang àt théhp เครื่องอัดเทป tape recorder

khrûeang àt widiioh เครื่องอัดวิดีโอ video recorder

khrûeang bin เครื่องบิน aeroplane

khrûeang càk เครื่องจักร machinery

khrûeang dùehm เครื่องดื่ม drink, refreshment

khrûeang fai fáa เครื่องไฟฟ้า appliance, electrical

khrûeang khǐan เครื่องเขียน stationery

khrûeang khít lêhk เครื่องคิดเลข calculator

khrûeang mueh เครื่องมือ tool, utensil, instrument

khrûeang nawn เครื่องนอน bedding, bedclothes

khrûeang phét phlawi เครื่องเพชรพลอย jewelry

khrûeang pradàp kai เครื่องประดับกาย body ornaments

khrûeang pradàp sǐisà เครื่องประดับศีรษะ headdress

khrûeang ráp thohrasàp เครื่องรับโทรศัพท์ answering machine

khrûeang thêht เครื่องเทศ spices

khrûeang yon เครื่องยนต์ engine, machine

khruuu ครู teacher

khuai ควย penis (colloq.)

khuan ควร ought to, should

khùap ขวบ year of child's age

khùat ขวด bottle

khuehn คืน to give back, return

khuehn níi คืนนี้ tonight

khûen ขึ้น to rise, ascend, go up, upward; to board, get on (transport)

khûen yùu kàp ขึ้นอยู่กับ to depend on

khûen, yùu bon... ขึ้น, อยู่บน... on board

khûenchài ขึ้นใจ celery

khui คุย to chat

khúk คุก jail, prison

khúkkîi คุกกี้ cookie, sweet biscuit

khun คุณ you, (respectful address – like *Mr*, *Ms*)

khún khoei kàp... คุ้นเคยกับ... to be acquainted with...

khún khoei, chin คุ้นเคย, ชิน to be used to, accustomed

khun nai คุณนาย madam (term of address)

khun pâa คุณป้า aunt (respectful address to aging lady)

khunásǒmbàt คุณสมบัติ qualification, characteristic

khùu ขู่ to threaten

khûu คู่ pair

khûu khàeng คู่แข่ง rival

khûu mân คู่หมั้น fiancé, fiancée

khûu sǒmrót คู่สมรส partner, spouse

khuun คูณ times (multiplying)

khwǎa ขวา right (direction)

K

khwǎa mueh ขวามือ right-hand side

khwai ควาย water buffalo

khwaam... ความ... ...ness, essence (abstract to noun)

khwaam campen ความจำเป็น need, necessity

khwaam cèp pùai ความเจ็บป่วย illness

khwaam chûai lǔea ความช่วยเหลือ assistance

khwaam chûea ความเชื่อ belief, faith

khwaam cing ความจริง truth, the truth is, actually

khwaam fǎn ความฝัน dream

khwaam hàang klai ความห่างไกล distance

khwaam hěn ความเห็น opinion

khwaam ìtchǎa ความอิจฉา jealousy

khwaam khaoróp ความเคารพ respect

khwaam khít ความคิด idea, thoughts

khwaam khlûean wǎy ความเคลื่อนไหว movement, motion

khwaam khun khoei ความคุ้นเคย acquaintance

khwaam klìat ความเกลียด hatred

khwaam klua ความกลัว fear

khwaam kòt dan ความกดดัน pressure

khwaam kròht ความโกรธ anger

khwaam kwâang ความกว้าง width

khwaam lambàak ความลำบาก trouble

khwaam láp ความลับ secret

khwaam lóm lěo ความล้มเหลว failure

khwaam mǎi ความหมาย meaning

khwaam mâi sangòp ความไม่สงบ disturbance

khwaam mâncai ความมั่นใจ confidence

khwaam òp ùn ความอบอุ่น warmth

khwaam òt yàak ความอดอยาก famine

khwaam phayaayaam ความพยายาม attempt, effort

khwaam phìt ความผิด fault, mistake, error

khwaam praathanǎa ความปรารถนา desire

khwaam rák ความรัก love

khwaam rák khrâi ความรักใคร่ affection

khwaam ráp phìt châwp ความรับผิดชอบ responsibility

khwaam ráp rúu ความรับรู้ awareness

khwaam reo ความเร็ว speed

khwaam rúu ความรู้ knowledge

khwaam rúusùek ความรู้สึก feeling

khwaam sa-àat ความสะอาด cleanliness

khwaam sǎmkhan ความสำคัญ importance

khwaam sǎmrèt ความสำเร็จ success

khwaam sǒncai ความสนใจ interest (personal)

khwaam song cam ความทรงจำ memories

khwaam sǒngsǎi ความสงสัย suspicion

khwaam sǔung ความสูง height

khwaam tàehk tàang ความแตกต่าง difference (in quality)

khwaam tai ความตาย death

khwaam tângcai ความตั้งใจ intention

khwaam thâo thiam ความเท่าเทียม equality

khwaam yao ความยาว length

khwâang ขว้าง to throw

khwǎang thaang ขวางทาง bar (blocking way)

khwâang thíng ขว้างทิ้ง throw away, throw out

khwǎehn แขวน to hang

khwan ควัน smoke

kìao kàp เกี่ยวกับ about, regarding, concerning

kìao khâwng เกี่ยวข้อง to involve

kìi... กี่... how many...?

kíi, kîi... กี้... a moment ago

kìi mohng láeo กี่โมงแล้ว what time?

kiilaa กีฬา sports

kìit khwǎang กีดขวาง to hinder

kiiwii frút กีวีฟรุต kiwi fruit

kiloh(kram) กิโล(กรัม) kilogram
kiloh(méht) กิโล(เมตร) kilometer
kin กิน to eat
kin aahǎan cháo กินอาหารเช้า
eat breakfast
kin ceh กินเจ tọ be vegetarian
kìng mái กิ่งไม้ tree branch
kìtcakam กิจกรรม activity
klâa haǎn กล้าหาญ brave, daring
klâam núea กล้ามเนื้อ muscle
klaang กลาง middle, center, to be in
the middle of doing something
klaang khuehn กลางคืน night
klaang mueang กลางเมือง city/town
center
klaang wan กลางวัน day
klâehng แกล้ง to pretend
klai ไกล far
klâi ใกล้ close to, nearby
klai pen กลายเป็น to become
klâi wehlaa ใกล้เวลา to approach
(in time)
klào hǎa กล่าวหา to accuse
klào kham praasǎi กล่าวคำปราศรัย to
make a speech
klào thǔeng กล่าวถึง to mention
klàp กลับ to turn over
klàp bâan กลับบ้าน to return home,
go home
klàp khâang กลับข้าง reversed,
backwards
klàp maa กลับมา to come back
klàp pai กลับไป to return, go back
klâwng กล้อง camera
klàwng กล่อง box
klàwng kradàat กล่องกระดาษ
cardboard box
klìat เกลียด to hate
klìn กลิ่น smell
klom กลม round (shape)
klua กลัว afraid
klûai กล้วย banana
kluea เกลือ salt
kluehn กลืน to swallow

klùm กลุ่ม group
klûm cai กลุ้มใจ to worry
koehn เกิน to exceed
koehn pai ...เกินไป too...(excessive)
kòeht เกิด to be born
kòeht arai khûen เกิดอะไรขึ้น
happened, what happened?
kòeht khûen เกิดขึ้น happen, occur
kohhòk โกหก to lie, tell a falsehood
kohn โกน to shave
kohng โกง to cheat
kôn ก้น bottom, buttocks
kòt กฎ rules
kòt กด to press
kòt kring กดกริ่ง to ring (bell)
kòtmǎi กฎหมาย laws, legislation
kraam กราม jaw
krabuai กระบวย ladle, dipper
kracai sǐang กระจายเสียง
to broadcast
kracòk กระจก glass (material), mirror
kradaan กระดาน board, plank
kradaan prakàat กระดานประกาศ
signboard
kradàat กระดาษ paper
kradàat khǎeng กระดาษแข็ง
cardboard
kradòht กระโดด to jump
kradùuk กระดูก bone
kradùuk sǎn lang กระดูกสันหลัง spine
krapǎo กระเป๋า luggage, pocket
krapǎo doehn thaang กระเป๋าเดินทาง
baggage
krapǎo ngoen กระเป๋าเงิน purse (for
money)
krapǎo sataang, krapǎo tang กระเป๋า
สตางค์ wallet
krapǎo sûea phâa กระเป๋าเสื้อผ้า
suitcase
krapǎo tham ngaan กระเป๋าทำงาน
briefcase
krapǎwng กระป๋อง can, tin, bucket
kraprohng กระโปรง skirt
krathâwm กระท่อม hut, shack

K

K

krathiam กระเทียม garlic

kratùk กระตุก to stall a vehicle

kràwk (bàehp) fawm กรอกแบบฟอร์ม fill out a form

krehngcai เกรงใจ feeling of owing in return, of imposing on someone

kreng เกร็ง tense

kròht โกรธ upset, cross, angry

kruai kliao กรวย เกลียว spiral

krung กรุง city

krungthêhp กรุงเทพฯ Bangkok (city of angels)

kúai tíao ก๋วยเตี๋ยว noodles

kùeap เกือบ almost, nearly

kumphaaphan กุมภาพันธ์ February

kuncaeh กุญแจ key (to room)

kûng กุ้ง shrimp, prawn

kwàa กว่า more (comparative), than

kwâang กว้าง broad, spacious, wide

kwàat กวาด to sweep

kwàeng แกว่ง to swing

L

lâ ล่ะ *end particle*: and what about...?

lá, la ละ per, each one

lá-ai ละอาย shame, disgrace

lâa cháa ล่าช้า delayed

laa kàwn ลาก่อน goodbye

lâa sùt ล่าสุด at the latest

lâam ล่าม interpreter

láan ล้าน million

lǎan หลาน grandchild, niece, nephew

lǎan chai หลานชาย grandson, nephew

lǎan sǎo หลานสาว granddaughter, niece

lâang ล่าง below

láang ล้าง to develop film, to wash

láang caan ล้างจาน wash the dishes

lâat khǎo ลาดเขา slope

lâatkrabang ลาดกระบัง Latkrabang, area 33 km east of Bangkok center

lâatphráo ลาดพร้าว Latprao, area 12 km NE of Bangkok center

láe และ and

lâehk chék แลกเช็ค to cash a check

lâehk plìan แลกเปลี่ยน to trade, exchange

lâehk plìan ngoen แลกเปลี่ยนเงิน to exchange money

lâehp แลบ to flash (like lightning)

lâen ruea แล่นเรือ to sail

láeo แล้ว already; then, and then

lǎi ไหล to flow

lǎi หลาย several

lâi àwk ไล่ออก to fire someone

lai màak rúk ลายหมากรุก checked (pattern)

lâi pai ไล่ไป to chase away, chase out

lǎi sìp หลายสิบ tens of, multiples of ten

lâi taam ไล่ตาม to chase after

laisen ลายเซ็น signature

lák lâwp ลักลอบ to smuggle

làk mueang หลักเมือง Lakmuang, the city pillar

lakhawn ละคร play, theatrical production

làkthǎn, khrûeang phísùut หลักฐาน, เครื่องพิสูจน์ proof

lá-loei, mâai rúu rûeang ละเลย, ไม่รู้เรื่อง ignorant

lambàak ลำบาก troublesome

lamyai ลำไย longan

lǎng หลัง back (part of body), back, rear

lǎng càak หลังจาก after

lǎng càak nán หลังจากนั้น afterwards, then

lang mái ลังไม้ crate

lǎngkhaa หลังคา roof

lao ลาว Laos, Lao

lâo เล่า to tell a story, relate

lâo เหล้า spirits, liquor, alcohol

làp หลับ to sleep

lathí chintoh ลัทธิชินโต Shintoism

lathí hǐnayaan ลัทธิหินยาน Lesser vehicle of Buddhism, Hinayana

lathí hinduu ลัทธิฮินดู Hinduism

lathí khaathawlík ลัทธิคาทอลิค Roman Catholic

lathí khŏng cúeh ลัทธิขงจื๊อ Confucianism

lathí mahǎayaan ลัทธิมหายาน Greater vehicle of Buddhism, Mahayana

lathí prohtaehsatâen ลัทธิโปรเตสแตนท์ Protestant

lathí tǎo ลัทธิเต๋า Taoism

làw หล่อ handsome

láw ล้อ wheel

làwk หลอก *end particle*: on the contrary

láwk ล็อค to lock

láwk láeo ล็อคแล้ว locked

làwk luang หลอกลวง to deceive

lawng ลอง to try out

lawng sài ลองใส่ try on (clothes)

láwttoehrîi ล็อตเตอรี่ lottery

lêhk เลข number

lehkhǎanúkaan เลขานุการ secretary

lehn เลน lane (of a highway)

lék เล็ก little, small

lèk เหล็ก iron, metal

lèk klâa เหล็กกล้า steel

lék náwi เล็กน้อย slight, tiny

lékchôeh เล็คเชอร์ lecturer (at university)

lêm เล่ม *classifier* for books and knives

lên เล่น to play

lên ngao เล่นเงา to shadow play

lên pai thûa เล่นไปทั่ว to play around

lên tôh khlûehn เล่นโต้คลื่น surf

leo เลว bad

lěo เหลว liquid-like

lép เล็บ fingernail, toenail

lia เลีย to lick

lǐan เหรียญ dollar (dialectal form, see **rǐan**)

líang เลี้ยง to bring up, raise (children or animals); to treat (something special), pay for food or drinks

líao เลี้ยว to turn, make a turn

líao klàp เลี้ยวกลับ to turn around

líf ลิฟต์ lift, elevator

lín ลิ้น tongue

línchák ลิ้นชัก drawer

líncìi ลิ้นจี่ lychee

ling ลิง monkey, ape

lít ลิตร litre

lǒeh หรือ really?, is that so?; *end particle*: question word asks for confirmation (perhaps with some doubt or surprise)

lôehk เลิก to cease

lôehk kan เลิกกัน broken off a relationship

loei เลย therefore, so, beyond; (intensifies adjective), ... at all

lǒh โหล dozen

lôhk โลก Earth, the world

lom ลม wind, breeze

lôm ล่ม overturned (boat)

lóm ล้ม to topple, fall over

long ลง to go downwards; to land (plane), get off (transport)

lǒng (thaang) หลง (ทาง) lost (can't find the way)

long khanaehn sǐang ลงคะแนนเสียง to vote

long maa ลงมา down, downward

long thabian ลงทะเบียน to register

lóp ลบ less, minus; to wipe out

lót ลด to reduce, lower

lót long ลดลง decrease, lessen, reduce

lót námnàk ลดน้ำหนัก to diet, lose weight

lót raakhaa ลดราคา (to) discount, sale (reduced prices)

lǔam หลวม loose (wobbly, not tight)

lúang krapǎo ล้วงกระเป๋า to pickpocket

lûat ลวด wire

lǔea เหลือ to be left over

L

lúeai เลื้อย to crawl
lûeak เลือก to pick, choose, select
lûeak dâi เลือกได้ optional
lûean เลื่อน to put off, delay
lûean àwk pai เลื่อนออกไป
   postponed, delayed
lŭeang เหลือง yellow
lûeat เลือด blood
luehm ลืม to leave behind by
   accident, forget
luehm kìao kàp... ลืมเกี่ยวกับ...
   to forget about...
lûehn ลื่น to slip, slippery
lúek ลึก deep
lúek láp ลึกลับ myth
lúk khûen ลุกขึ้น get up (from bed)
lŭm sòp หลุมศพ grave
lung ลุง uncle, either parent's older
   brother
lûuk ลูก child (offspring); *classifier*
   for small round objects eg. fruit,
   marbles
lûuk anthá ลูกอัณฑะ testicles
lûuk chaii ลูกชาย son
lûuk chín ลูกชิ้น meatball
lûuk kháa ลูกค้า customer
lûuk khŏei ลูกเขย son-in-law
lûuk khrûeng ลูกครึ่ง
   person of mixed race
lûuk lăan ลูกหลาน descendants
lûuk náwng ลูกน้อง employee
lûuk plam ลูกพลัม plum
lûuk săo ลูกสาว daughter
lûuk saphái ลูกสะใภ้ daughter-in-law

M

maa มา to come; *also indicates*
   time up to the present, direction
   incoming
mŭa หมา dog
máa ม้า horse
maa càak มาจาก originate, come
   from

maa cawng มาจอง mah jong
maa thŭeng มาถึง to arrive at
mâak kwàa มากกว่า more of (things)
màak rúk หมากรุก chess
mâak thîi sùt มากที่สุด most (the
   most of)
maalehsia มาเลเซีย Malaysia,
   Malaysian
mâan ม่าน curtains, drapes
maarayâat dii มารยาทดี
   well-mannered
mâeh แม่ mother
mâeh khrua แม่ครัว cook (female)
mâeh kuncaeh แม่กุญแจ lock
mâeh mâi แม่ม่าย widow
mâeh náam แม่น้ำ river
mâeh săamii แม่สามี mother-in-law
máeh tàeh แม้แต่ even (also)
máeh wâa แม้ว่า though
mâeh yai แม่ยาย mother-in-law
maeo แมว cat
mahăa samùt มหาสมุทร ocean
mahăa wítthayaalai มหาวิทยาลัย
   university
mài ใหม่ new
mâi ม่าย widowed
mâi ไหม้ to burn
mâi ไม่ no, not (with verbs and
   adjectives)
mái ไม้ wood
mái ไหม *end particle*:
   question word asking opinion
măi ไหม silk
mâi campen ไม่จำเป็น unnecessary
mâi châwp ไม่ชอบ to dislike
mâi...kâw... ไม่...ก็... either...or
mâi khâwi mii ไม่ค่อยมี
   hard to find, scarce
mâi khít ngoen ไม่คิดเงิน
   free of charge
mâi khoei ไม่เคย never
mâi khrâi ca ไม่ใคร่จะ seldom, rarely
măi khwaam หมายความ to mean
mâi kìi... ไม่กี่... few...

mái kwàat ไม้กวาด broom

mǎi lêhk thohrasàp หมายเลขโทรศัพท์ telephone number

mâi mâak mâi náwi ไม่มากไม่น้อย more or less

mâi mii ไม่มี no, not (with nouns)

mâi mii arai ไม่มีอะไร nothing

mâi mii khâw phùuk mát ไม่มีข้อผูกมัด free of commitments

mâi mii khrai ไม่มีใคร nobody

mâi mii khwaam sùk ไม่มีความสุข unhappy

mâi mii prayòht ไม่มีประโยชน์ useless

mâi mii thîi nǎi ไม่มีที่ไหน nowhere

mâi mòt ไหม้หมด burned down, out

mâi pen rai ไม่เป็นไร don't mention it!, never mind!, you're welcome!, it doesn't matter, it's nothing

mâi phaehng ไม่แพง inexpensive

mâi phèt ไม่เผ็ด mild (not spicy)

mây phiang...tàeh yang... ไม่เพียง...แต่ยัง... not only...but also

mâi prasòp phǒn sǎmrèt ไม่ประสบผลสำเร็จ to fail

mâi run raehng ไม่รุนแรง mild (not severe)

mâi sabai cai ไม่สบายใจ upset, unhappy

mâi sǎmkhan ไม่สำคัญ minor (not important)

mái sǎo ไม้เสา stick, pole

mái sìap ไม้เสียบ skewer

mâi sùk ไม่สุก unripe

mâi sùphâap ไม่สุภาพ impolite

mâi tháng ไม่ทั้ง neither

máikhìit ไม้ขีด matches

màk หมาก betel nut (chewed)

mâk มาก many, much, quite (very), extremely

mák ca... มักจะ... usually, regularly

màk faràng หมากฝรั่ง chewing gum

mâk koehn pai มากเกินไป too much

makhǔea thêht มะเขือเทศ tomato

makhǔea yao มะเขือยาว aubergine, eggplant

malaehng แมลง insect

malaehng wan แมลงวัน fly (insect)

malákaw มะละกอ papaya, pawpaw

mamûang มะม่วง mango

man มัน it; potato-like vegetables; shiny, brilliant

man มัน excellent, most enjoyable

mân หมั้น engaged (to be married)

man faràng มันฝรั่ง potatoes

man thêht มันเทศ yams

manao มะนาว lemon, lime (citrus fruit)

mâng khâng มั่งคั่ง wealthy

mangkhút มังคุด mangosteen

mangsa-wírát มังสวิรัติ vegetarian

mânkhong มั่นคง to be firm, definite, secure, safe

manút มนุษย์ human

mao เมา drunk

máo เมาส์ mouse (computer)

máphráo มะพร้าว coconut

maruehn níi มะรืนนี้ day after tomorrow

mâw หม้อ pan, pot

mǎw หมอ doctor

màwk หมอก mist, fog

mǎwn หมอน pillow

mawng มอง watch, look, see

mawnítôeh มอนิเตอร์ monitor (of computer)

mâwp hâi มอบให้ hand over

mawtôeh, khrûeang yon มอเตอร์, เครื่องยนต์ motor, engine

mawtoehsai มอเตอร์ไซค์ motorcycle

maẁ-sǒm เหมาะสม suitable, fitting, compatible, appropriate

mêhk mâak เมฆมาก overcast, cloudy

mehnuu เมนู menu

mehsǎayon เมษายน April

méht เมตร metre

měn เหม็น to stink

mét

mét เม็ด seed ; *classifier* for small seed-like objects, e.g. pillu

mia เมีย wife (street term)

mia náwi เมียน้อย mistress

mii มี to have, own; there is, there are

mii... hâi มี ... ให้ available

mii amnâat มีอำนาจ powerful

mii cèhtanaa มีเจตนา to mean, intend

mii chiiwít มีชีวิต live (be alive)

mii itthíphon มีอิทธิพล to influence

mii khâa มีค่า to be worth

mii khon thoh maa มีคนโทร.มา call on the telephone

mii khun khâa มีคุณค่า value, good

mii khwaam mâncai มีความมั่นใจ to have confidence

mii khwaam sùk มีความสุข happy

mii klìn มีกลิ่น odor, bad smell

mii lai มีลาย patterned, striped

mii phít มีพิษ poisonous

mii phòn tàw มีผลต่อ... to affect

mii pracam duean มีประจำเดือน to menstruate

mii prasòpkaan มีประสบการณ์ to experience

mii prayòht มีประโยชน์ useful

mii samaathí มีสมาธิ to concentrate, think deeply

mii sùan rûam มีส่วนร่วม to participate

mii tháksà มีทักษะ skilful

miinaakhom มีนาคม March

mîit มีด knife

mínâalâ มิน่าล่ะ no wonder!

minburii มีนบุรี Minburi, area 27 km ENE of Bangkok center

míthùnaayon มิถุนายน June

moehl aakàat เมล์อากาศ airmail

moehnchòehi เมินเฉย to ignore

mohhòh โมโห cross, angry

mohng โมง o'clock

mókkaraakhom มกราคม January

mòt aayú หมดอายุ past its use-by date, worn out (machine)

mòt láeo หมดแล้ว finished (none left), all gone

mót lûuk มดลูก uterus

mòt raehng หมดแรง puffed out, tired

muai thai มวยไทย Thai boxing

mùak หมวก hat

mûang ม่วง purple

mûea khuehn níi เมื่อคืนนี้ last night

mûea kîi níi เมื่อกี้นี้ a moment ago

mûea waan níi เมื่อวานนี้ yesterday

mûea waan suehn níi เมื่อวานซืนนี้ day before yesterday

mùean เหมือน to resemble, be similar to, like, as

mueang เมือง town, city

mueang ciin เมืองจีน China

mueang thai เมืองไทย Thailand

mùeankan เหมือนกัน identical, likewise

mûearai kâw dâi เมื่อไรก็ได้ whenever, any time

mûearài, mûearai เมื่อไหร่ when?

mueh มือ hand

múeh มื้อ meal

mueh thùeh มือถือ cell phone, mobile phone

mùehn หมื่น ten thousand

mûeht มืด dark

mûeht khrúem มืดครึ้ม cloudy, overcast

mùek หมึก ink

mum มุม corner

mùn หมุน to dial, ring (telephone)

mùn thohrásàp หมุนโทรศัพท์ to dial the telephone

múng มุ้ง mosquito net

múng lûat มุ้งลวด fly screen

mûng pai มุ่งไป head for, toward

mútsalim, múslim มุสลิม Muslim

mùu หมู pig

mùu bâan หมู่บ้าน village

22

N

ná นะ *end particle*: with me?, catch what I'm saying?

naa นา paddy, rice field

nâa หน้า face, page, front (ahead)

năa หนา thick (of things)

náa น้า aunt (younger than mother)

nâa antarai น่าอันตราย dangerous

nâa bùea น่าเบื่อ boring, dull

nâa chûea fang น่าเชื่อฟัง obedient

nâa dueng dùut น่าดึงดูด attractive

nâa ìtchăa น่าอิจฉา envious

nâa kàak หน้ากาก mask

nâa khăi nâa น่าขายหน้า shame: what a shame!

nâa klìat น่าเกลียด ugly

nâa klua น่ากลัว scary, frightening

nâa lá-ai น่าละอาย ashamed, embarrassed, embarrassing

nâa năo หน้าหนาว winter

nâa òk หน้าอก breast(s), chest

nâa phàak หน้าผาก forehead

nâa plàehk caa น่าแปลกใจ surprising

nâa pralàat cai น่าประหลาดใจ wonderful

nâa rák น่ารัก cute, appealing, lovely, pretty

nâa rák mâak น่ารักมาก very pretty

nâa rangkìat น่ารังเกียจ disgusting

nâa ráwn หน้าร้อน summer

nâa sanùk น่าสนุก enjoyable

nâa sàpsŏn น่าสับสน confusing

nâa sŏncai น่าสนใจ interesting

nâa sŏngsăan น่าสงสาร pity: what a pity!

nâa tàang หน้าต่าง window (in house)

nâa thîi หน้าที่ duty (responsibility)

nâa tùehn tên น่าตื่นเต้น exciting

nâa yindii น่ายินดี pleasant

naalíkaa นาฬิกา wristwatch, clock; o'clock for 24 hour system

náam น้ำ water (*also see* entries under **nám** ...)

náam àt lom น้ำอัดลม soft drink

náam phú น้ำพุ spring (of water)

náam phú ráwn น้ำพุร้อน hot spring

naam sakun นามสกุล surname

náam thûam น้ำท่วม flood

naan นาน long (time)

naan thâorai นานเท่าไร how long?

naanaachâat นานาชาติ international

nâatàang หน้าต่าง window

naathii นาที minute

naayók rathamondrii นายกรัฐมนตรี prime minister

nâen แน่น crowded, solid, tight

nâeh cai แน่ใจ certain, sure

nâeh nawn แน่นอน certainly!, of course, exact, exactly

náenam แนะนำ to advise, recommend, suggest

náenam tua แนะนำตัว to introduce someone

náenam tua ehng แนะนำตัวเอง to introduce oneself

naeo แนว stripe, line

nai นาย boss, Mr

nai ใน in, at (space)

năi ไหน which?

nai adìit ในอดีต pastime

nai anaakhót ในอนาคต future: in future

nai mâi cháa ในไม่ช้า soon

nai mueang ในเมือง downtown, urban

nai thîi sùt ในที่สุด finally

nailawn ไนลอน nylon

nàk หนัก heavy

nák bin นักบิน aeroplane pilot

nák doehn thaang นักเดินทาง traveler

nák khào นักข่าว journalist

nák khǐan นักเขียน writer

nák lúang krapăo นักล้วงกระเป๋า pickpocket

nák rian นักเรียน pupil

nák thâwng thîao นักท่องเที่ยว tourist

THAI–ENGLISH

N

nák thurákìt นักธุรกิจ businessperson

nákrian นักเรียน student

nam นำ to guide, lead

nám chaa น้ำชา tea

nám cîm น้ำจิ้ม sauce (chili)

nám hăwm น้ำหอม perfume

nám khăeng น้ำแข็ง ice

nam khâo นำเข้า to import

nam pai นำไป lead (to guide someone somewhere)

nám phŏnlamái น้ำผลไม้ juice

nám phûeng น้ำผึ้ง honey

nám plaa น้ำปลา fish sauce

nám sôm น้ำส้ม orange juice

nám sôm săi chuu น้ำส้มสายชู vinegar

nám súp น้ำซุป soup, broth

nám taa น้ำตา tears

nám tòk น้ำตก waterfall

námman น้ำมัน gasoline, petrol

námman khrûeang น้ำมันเครื่อง engine oil

námman ngaa น้ำมันงา sesame oil

námnàk น้ำหนัก weight

námnàk khûen น้ำหนักขึ้น to gain weight

námnàk lót น้ำหนักลด to lose weight

námtaan น้ำตาล brown (colour), sugar

nân làe นั่นแหละ exactly! just so!

nán, lào nán นั้น, เหล่านั้น that, those

nâng นั่ง to sit

năng หนัง film, movie

năng หนัง leather

nâng long นั่งลง to sit down

nâng rót นั่งรถ ride (in car)

nangsǔeh หนังสือ book

nangsǔeh doehn thaang หนังสือเดินทาง passport

nangsǔeh nam thîao หนังสือนำเที่ยว guidebook

nangsǔeh phim หนังสือพิมพ์ newspaper

nâo เน่า rotten

năo หนาว cold weather, cold in body temperature

năo sàn หนาวสั่น to shiver

năo yen หนาวเย็น chilled

náp นับ count, reckon

nápthǔeh นับถือ to respect

nát นัด to fix/set a time, make an appointment

nátmăi นัดหมาย appointment

nàw mái หน่อไม้ bamboo shoots

náwi น้อย little (not much)

náwi kwàa น้อยกว่า less (smaller amount)

náwi thîi sùt น้อยที่สุด least (smallest amount)

náwi-nàa น้อยหน่า custard apple

nâwk นอก outside

nâwk càak นอกจาก apart, besides, except

nâwk càak níi นอกจากนี้ besides this, for another thing

nâwk càak wâa นอกจากว่า unless

nawn นอน to lie down

nawn làp นอนหลับ asleep, to sleep

nâwng น่อง calf (lower leg)

náwng น้อง younger brother or sister

náwng chai น้องชาย younger brother

náwng khŏei น้องเขย younger brother-in-law

náwng mia น้องเมีย wife's younger sibling

náwng săamii น้องสามี husband's younger sibling

náwng săo น้องสาว younger sister

náwng saphái น้องสะใภ้ younger sister-in-law

na-wa-níyai นวนิยาย novel

nékthai เน็คไท necktie

ngaa งา sesame seeds

ngaa cháang งาช้าง ivory

ngaan งาน job, work; party, ceremony

ngaan adirèhk งานอดิเรก hobby

P

ngaan fĭimueh งานฝีมือ crafts
ngaan líang งานเลี้ยง banquet
ngaan sòp งานศพ funeral
ngaan tàeng ngaan งานแต่งงาน
  wedding
ngâi ง่าย simple, easy
ngǎi tháwng หงายท้อง overturned,
  upside down
ngán งั้น in that case
ngán ngán งั้นๆ average (so-so, just
  okay)
ngao เงา shadow
ngǎo เหงา lonely
ngáw เงาะ rambutan
ngîap เงียบ quiet, silent, still
ngoen เงิน money, silver
ngoen cài เงินจ่าย payment
ngoen duean เงินเดือน salary
ngoen fàak เงินฝาก deposit
  (put money in the bank)
ngoen mát cam เงินมัดจำ advance
  money, deposit
ngoen sòt เงินสด cash, money
ngoen traa เงินตรา currency
ngôh โง่ stupid
ngong งง puzzled
ngong nguai งงงวย confused
  (mentally)
ngûang ง่วง sleepy, tired
ngùea เหงื่อ sweat
ngùea àwk เหงื่อออก to perspire,
  sweat
ngûean khǎi เงื่อนไข
  condition (pre-condition)
nguu งู snake
nian rîap เนียนเรียบ
  smooth (of surfaces)
nĭao เหนียว sticky
nîi นี่ here
nîi sĭn หนี้สิน debt
níi, lào níi นี้, เหล่านี้ this, these
nîng นิ่ง still, quiet
nít nàwi นิดหน่อย slightly, a little bit
níu นิ้ว finger

niusiilaehn นิวซีแลนด์ New Zealand
noei เนย butter
noei khǎeng เนยแข็ง cheese
noehn khǎo เนินเขา hill
nôhn โน่น yonder, over there
nóhn โน้น that over there
nók นก bird
nom นม milk; breasts
nontháburii นนทบุรี Nonthaburi,
  provincial capital 10 km north of
  Bangkok center on the east bank
  of the Chaopraya river
nûat นวด to massage
nùat หนวด moustache
núea เนื้อ beef, meat
nŭea เหนือ north
núea kàe เนื้อแกะ lamb, mutton
núea mŭu เนื้อหมู pork
nùeai เหนื่อย physically tired, weary
núek นึก to recall, think
nùeng หนึ่ง one (cardinal number)
nûeng นึ่ง steamed
nùeng khûu หนึ่งคู่ pair of, a
nùeng thii หนึ่งที once
nûm นุ่ม soft
nùm sǎo หนุ่มสาว youths (teenagers)
nǔu หนู mouse (animal), rat

O

ôh hoh โอ้โฮ goodness!
ohkàat โอกาส chance, opportunity
ohlíang โอเลี้ยง iced black coffee
ohyúa โอยัวะ hot black coffee
ongsǎa องศา degrees (temperature)
òp อบ to bake, baked
òp ùn อบอุ่น warm
òt aahǎan อดอาหาร to fast
òt thon อดทน patient (calm)

P

pàa ป่า forest, jungle
pàa ป่า wild (of animals)

P

pâa ป้า aunt, either parent's older sister

pàak ปาก mouth

pàakkaa ปากกา pen

pàakkaa mùek hâehng ปากกาหมึกแห้ง ballpoint

pàakkaa mùek suem ปากกาหมึกซึม fountain pen

pàakkrèt ปากเกร็ด Pakkret, area 16 km north of Bangkok center

pâehn แป้น key (computer)

pâehng แป้ง flour, (talcum) powder

pâehng yát sây núea แป้งยัดไส้เนื้อ dumpling (meat)

pàeht แปด eight

pàeht sìp แปดสิบ eighty

pai ไป to go; also indicates time from now on; direction outgoing; beyond expectation, as in **phaehng pai** = too expensive

pai ao maa ไปเอามา to fetch, go and get

pai doehn lên ไปเดินเล่น go for a walk

pai dûai ไปด้วย to go along, join in

pai kan ไปกัน come on, let's go

pai khâng nâa ไปข้างหน้า to go forward

pai nawn ไปนอน to go to bed

pai pen phûean ไปเป็นเพื่อน to accompany

pâi sathǎanii ป้าย สถานี stop (bus, train)

pai sòng ไปส่ง give a lift, see off

pai sùu ไปสู่ toward

pai súeh khǎwng ไปซื้อของ to shop, go shopping

pai thátsaná-cawn ไปทัศนาจร sightseeing

pai thîi nǎi ไปที่ไหน where to?

pai yang ไปยัง to, toward (a place)

pai yîam ไปเยี่ยม to go around, pay a visit

pàk ปัก embroidered

pám námman ปั๊มน้ำมัน gasoline/petrol station

pân ปั้น to sculpt

panhǎa ปัญหา problem

pào เป่า to blow

pâo mǎi เป้าหมาย goal

pàtcùban níi ปัจจุบันนี้ presently, nowadays

pathumwan ปทุมวัน Pathumwan, area 2 km ESE of Bangkok center

patìbàt ปฏิบัติ to operate, perform

patìbàt tàw nâa thîi ปฏิบัติต่อหน้าที่ to perform one's duty/function

patìbàt tàw, tham tàw ปฏิบัติต่อ, ทำต่อ to treat, behave towards

patìsèht ปฏิเสธ to decline, refuse

pàwk ปอก to peel

pàwt ปอด lungs

pâwm ป้อม fortress

pâwm pràap ป้อมปราบ Pomprab, area 2 km NE of Bangkok center

pawn ปอนด์ pound (money)

pâwn ป้อน to feed someone

pâwng kan ป้องกัน to prevent; defend (in war)

pêh เป๋ military-style cloth bag

pen เป็น to be someone or something; to know how to do something

pen câo khǎwng เป็นเจ้าของ to own, possess

pen hèht hâi เป็นเหตุให้ to be the cause, reason

pen ìtsarà เป็นอิสระ to have freedom, be loose

pen kan ehng เป็นกันเอง to be friendly, outgoing

pen khǎwng เป็นของ to belong to

pen ngao เป็นเงา shiny

pen nîi เป็นหนี้ to owe, be in debt to

pen pai dâi เป็นไปได้ to be possible

pen pai mâi dâi เป็นไปไม่ได้ to be impossible

pen phǒn maa càak... เป็นผลมาจาก...
resulting from, as a result
pen rabìap เป็นระเบียบ to be orderly,
organized
pen thammachâat เป็นธรรมชาติ
to be natural
pen thammadaa เป็นธรรมดา
to be typical, normal
pen thîi níyom เป็นที่นิยม
to be popular
pen thîi phaw cai เป็นที่พอใจ
to be satisfied
pèt เป็ด duck
phaa พา to take someone
somewhere
phàa ผ่า to split
phâa ผ้า fabric, textile, cloth
phâa chét tua ผ้าเช็ดตัว towel
phâa hòm ผ้าห่ม blanket
phâa khîi ríu ผ้าขี้ริ้ว tripe
phâa mâan ผ้าม่าน curtains
phâa puu ผ้าปู sheet (for bed)
phâa puu tó ผ้าปูโต๊ะ tablecloth
phâa puu thîi nawn ผ้าปูที่นอน
bedsheet
phâa sîn ผ้าซิ่น
Thai long one-piece skirt
phâak bangkháp ภาคบังคับ
compulsory
phàan ผ่าน to pass, go past;
via, through
phâap kwâang ภาพกว้าง panorama
phâap wâat ภาพวาด painting
phaará ภาระ load
phaasǎa ภาษา language
phaasǎa angkrìt ภาษาอังกฤษ English
phaasǎa ciin ภาษาจีน
Chinese language
phaasǎa khaměhn/kamphuuchaa
ภาษาเขมร/กัมพูชา
Khmer/Cambodian language
phaasǎa thai ภาษาไทย
Thai language
phaasǎa thìn ภาษาถิ่น dialect

phaasǐi ภาษี rate, tariff, tax
phaasǐicharoehn ภาษีเจริญ
Phasicharoen, area on the west
bank 10 km SW of Bangkok
center
phaayú พายุ storm
phachoehn nâa เผชิญหน้า to face
pháe แพะ goat
pháeh แพ้ lose, be defeated;
to be allergic, sensitive to
phǎehn แผน plan
phǎehn thîi แผนที่ map
phàen แผ่น *classifier* for flat objects
eg. CDs, paper sheets
phàen din wǎi แผ่นดินไหว
earthquake
phàen dìs แผ่นดิสก์ diskette
phaeng แพง expensive
phai ภัย danger
phâi ไพ่ cards (game)
phai nai ภายใน in (time, years),
within
phai nai khâw camkàt ภายในข้อจำกัด
within reason
phai phíbàt ภัยพิบัติ disaster
phàk ผัก vegetable
phák พรรค party (political)
phàk chii ผักชี cilantro, coriander
phàk kàat khǎo ผักกาดขาว Chinese
cabbage
phàk khǒhm ผักโขม spinach
phák phàwn พักผ่อน to relax, rest
phàk sǐi khǐao ผักสีเขียว greens
phalaasatôeh pìt phlǎeh
พลาสเตอร์ปิดแผล bandage
phalìt ผลิต to manufacture,
produce
phamâa พม่า Burma, Burmese
phan พัน thousand
phan láan พันล้าน billion
phanàehk แผนก department
phanák-ngaan khǎi พนักงานขาย
sales assistant
phanrayaa, phanyaa ภรรยา wife

P

phào เผ่า tribal group

phǎo เผา to burn (to a cinder/crisp)

pháp พับ to fold

phasǒm ผสม to mix

phàt ผัด to stirfry

phátanaa พัฒนา to develop (happen)

phátlom พัดลม fan (for cooling)

phátsadù พัสดุ parcel

pháttaakhaan ภัตตาคาร restaurant (larger)

phaw พอ enough; as soon as, when

phâw พ่อ father

phaw cai พอใจ to be satisfied

phaw khuan พอควร quite (fairly)

phâw mâeh พ่อแม่ parents

phâw mâi พ่อม่าย widower

phaw sǎw พ.ศ. Buddhist era, BE

phaw sǒmkhuan พอสมควร reasonable (price)

phâw taa พ่อตา father-in-law

phǎwm ผอม thin (of persons), slim

phayaabaan พยาบาล nurse

phayaan พยาน witness

phayaathai พญาไท Phayathai, 7 km ENE from Bangkok center, includes Pratunam market

phayaayaam พยายาม to attempt, make an effort, try

phehdaan เพดาน ceiling

phêht เพศ gender, sex

phèt เผ็ด hot (spicy)

phét เพชร diamond

phǐi พี่ older brother or sister

phǐi ผี ghost

phǐi chai พี่ชาย older brother

phǐi khǒei พี่เขย older brother-in-law

phǐi mia พี่เมีย wife's older sibling

phǐi sǎamii พี่สามี husband's older sibling

phǐi sǎo พี่สาว older sister

phǐi saphái พี่สะใภ้ older sister-in-law

phǐi sûea ผีเสื้อ butterfly

phiang เพียง merely

phiang tàeh เพียงแต่ only

phícaaránaa พิจารณา to consider, have a considered opinion

phíkaan พิการ handicap

phim พิมพ์ to print, publish

phim dìit พิมพ์ดีด to type

phíphítthaphan พิพิธภัณฑ์ museum

phísèht พิเศษ special

phísùut พิสูจน์ to prove

phìt ผิด false (not true), guilty (of a crime), wrong (false)

phìt kòtmǎi ผิดกฎหมาย illegal

phìt phlâat ผิดพลาด mistaken

phìt wǎng ผิดหวัง disappointed

phíthii พิธี ceremony

phǐu ผิว skin, complexion

phlâat พลาด to be mistaken, make an error

phlǎeh แผล cut, wound

phlàk ผลัก to push

phlang ngaan พลังงาน energy

phlehng เพลง song

phóeh เพ้อ to be delirious

phôehm เพิ่ม to add, increase, extra

phôehm khûen เพิ่มขึ้น rise, increase

phôehm toehm เพิ่มเติม further, in addition

phôeng เพิ่ง just now

phol saowaroté ผลเสาวรส passionfruit

phǒm ผม hair

phǒm ผม I (male speaking)

phǒn ผล effect, result

phǒn tàang ผลต่าง difference (discrepancy in figures)

phǒng sák fâwk ผงซักฟอก detergent

phǒnlamái ผลไม้ fruit

phǒnprayòht ผลประโยชน์ profit

phóp พบ to find, meet

phóp kan mài พบกันใหม่ see you later!

phótcanaanúkrom พจนานุกรม dictionary

phrá พระ priest, monk

phrá aathít พระอาทิตย์ sun

phrá aathít khûen พระอาทิตย์ขึ้น sunrise

phrá aathít tòk พระอาทิตย์ตก sunset

phrá câo พระเจ้า god

phrá khanǒhng พระโขนง Phrakhanong, area south of Sukhumvit Road, 13 km ESE of Bangkok center

phrá mahâa-kasàt พระมหากษัตริย์ king

phrá nakhawn พระนคร Phranakhon, 1 km north of Bangkok center

phrá phûu pen câo พระผู้เป็นเจ้า God

phrárâatchawang พระราชวัง palace (royal)

phrarâatchinii พระราชินี queen

phráw เพราะ because; to sound nice

phráwm พร้อม ready

phrík พริก chilli pepper

phrík thai พริกไทย pepper, black

phrom พรม carpet

phrúetsacìkaayon พฤศจิกายน November

phrúetsaphaakhom พฤษภาคม May

phrûng níi พรุ่งนี้ tomorrow

phǔa ผัว husband (street term)

phûak พวก group

phûak kháo พวกเขา they, them

phuang พวง garland, cluster, bunch

phûang พ่วง in tow, connected

phûea arai เพื่ออะไร what for?

phûea thîi เพื่อที่ in order that, so that

phûea thîi ca... เพื่อที่จะ... so that...

phùea wâa เผื่อ in case

phùeak เผือก taro, tannia

phûean เพื่อน friend

phueân bâan เพื่อนบ้าน neighbor

phûean chai เพื่อนชาย boyfriend

phûean rûam ngaan เพื่อนร่วมงาน co-worker, colleague

phûean yǐng เพื่อนหญิง girlfriend

phúehn พื้น floor

phúehn din พื้นดิน land

phúehn phǐu พื้นผิว surface

phúehn thîi พื้นที่ area

phút พุทธ Buddhism

phûu aasǎi ผู้อาศัย resident, inhabitant

phûu amnuaikaan ผู้อำนวยการ director (of company)

phûu càtkaan ผู้จัดการ manager

phûu chai ผู้ชาย man

phûu chaná ผู้ชนะ winner

phûu doi sǎan ผู้โดยสาร passenger

phuu khǎo ภูเขา mountain

phuu khǎo fai ภูเขาไฟ volcano

phûu nam ผู้นำ leader

phûu phíphâaksǎa ผู้พิพากษา judge

phûu rai-ngaan ผู้รายงาน reporter

phûu yài ผู้ใหญ่ adult

phûu yǐng ผู้หญิง woman

phûu yùu aasǎi ผู้อยู่อาศัย inhabitant

phùuk ผูก to tie

phuumcai ภูมิใจ proud

phuumíphâak ภูมิภาค region

phûut พูด to speak, talk

phûut lên พูดเล่น joke

phûut rûeang พูดเรื่อง talk about

phûut wâa... พูดว่า... to say...

pìak เปียก wet

pii ปี years old, year; classes (at university) see also **rûn**

pii nâa ปีหน้า next year

pii thîi láeo ปีที่แล้ว last year

pìik ปีก wing

piin ปีน climb onto, into

pîng ปิ้ง grilled, toasted, to toast, grill

pìt ปิด to close, cover, shut; off, to turn something off

pìt láeo ปิดแล้ว turned off, closed

pìt pratuu ปิด ประตู to close the door

P

pìt ráan ปิด ร้าน to close shop
pìt thanŏn ปิด ถนน to close the road
plaa ปลา fish
plaa chalăam ปลาฉลาม shark
plaa mùek ปลาหมึก squid
plaasatìk, plaastìk พลาสติค plastic
plaeh แปล to translate
plaeh wâa... แปลว่า... it means...
plàehk แปลก strange
plàehk cai แปลกใจ surprised
plàehk nâa แปลกหน้า stranger
plai ปลาย end, tip
plai tháo ปลายเท้า toe
plák ปลั๊ก plug (bath)
plák fai ปลั๊กไฟ plug (electric)
plào เปล่า no (wrong assumption); empty
plàwi ปล่อย to release
plàwt phai ปลอดภัย safe
plàwt pròhng ปลอดโปร่ง clear (of weather)
plìan เปลี่ยน to change (conditions, situations), switch (clothes)
plìan cai เปลี่ยนใจ to change one's mind
plòt kasĭan ปลดเกษียณ retired
plueai เปลือย naked, nude
plùeak เปลือก shell, rind, peel
plùk ปลุก wake someone up
plùuk ปลูก to grow, cultivate, plant
poehsen เปอร์เซ็นต์ percent, percentage
pòeht เปิด on, to turn something on, switch on; open, to open; to reveal (make visible)
pòeht phŏei เปิดเผย reveal, to (make known)
pokkatì ปกติ regular, normal, usual
praakòt ปรากฏ appear, become visible
praasàat ปราสาท fortress, castle
praathanăa ปรารถนา to wish
pràatsacàak ปราศจาก without

pracam ประจำ regularly
pracam duean ประจำเดือน period (menstrual)
pracam pii ประจำปี annual
pracam sàpdaa ประจำสัปดาห์ weekly
pracam wan ประจำวัน daily
prachaachon ประชาชน citizen
pracaakawn ประชากร population
prachum ประชุม meeting
pradìt ประดิษฐ์ to invent, make up, create
praehng แปรง brush
praehng sĭi fan แปรงสีฟัน toothbrush
praisanii ไปรษณีย์ post office
praisanii thammadaa ไปรษณีย์ธรรมดา surface mail
praisaniiyábàt ไปรษณียบัตร postcard
prakàatsaniiyábàt ประกาศนียบัตร certificate
prakan ประกัน to guarantee; insurance, guarantee
prakàwp ประกอบ to assemble, put together
prakàwp dûai ประกอบด้วย made up of, comprising
pralàat cai ประหลาดใจ astonished
pramaan ประมาณ about, approximately, roughly; to estimate
pramuun ประมูล to auction
pramuun khăi ประมูลขาย auctioned off
pràp aakàat ปรับอากาศ air conditioning
praphêht ประเภท class, category, type
pràphrúet ประพฤติ behave
prasòpkaan ประสบการณ์ experience
prathaanaathíbàwdii ประธานาธิบดี president
pratháp cai ประทับใจ great, impressive
prathát ประทัด fireworks
prathêht ประเทศ country (nation)
prathúang ประท้วง to protest, go on strike

R

pratuu ประตู door, gate; goal in soccer

pra-wàt-sàat ประวัติศาสตร์ history

prayòhk ประโยค sentence

prîao เปรี้ยว sour; wild (of persons)

prîao wǎan เปรี้ยวหวาน sweet and sour

prìap kàp เปรียบกับ compared with

prìap thîap เปรียบเทียบ to compare

prùeksǎa ปรึกษา consult, talk over with

pùai ป่วย ill, sick

pùat ปวด to ache, be sore

puehn ปืน gun

pǔi ปุ๋ย fertilizer

pûm pûi ปุ้มปุ้ย stout (plump)

puu ปู crab

pùu ปู่ grandfather (paternal)

pùu yâa taa yai ปู่ย่าตายาย grandparents

R

râak ราก root (of plant)

raakhaa ราคา cost (price)

ráan ร้าน shop, store, vendor's stall

ráan aahǎan ร้านอาหาร restaurant

ráan khǎi yaa ร้านขายยา drugstore, pharmacy

ráan sǒehm sǔai ร้านเสริมสวย beauty parlor

râang kai ร่างกาย body

raangwan รางวัล prize, reward

râap ñap ราบเรียบ smooth (to go smoothly)

râap rûehn ราบรื่น harmonious

râat ราด to pour over, baste

rabai sǐi ระบายสี to paint

rabiang ระเบียง verandah, porch

rabìap ระเบียบ order, procedure, prospectus

rabòp iimeh(l) ระบบอีเมล์ email (system)

radàp ระดับ level (standard), degree

râehk แรก first

raehng แรง strength, force, power

rai ราย list

rái ร้าย wicked

rai cài รายจ่าย expense

rai chûeh รายชื่อ list

rái raehng ร้ายแรง serious (severe)

rái sǎará ไร้สาระ nonsense

raikaan รายการ list (of names)

raikaan aahǎan รายการอาหาร menu

raikaan choh รายการโชว์ show (broadcast)

raikaan kracai sǐang รายการกระจาย เสียง broadcast, program

raikaan sòt รายการสด show (live performance)

raì-ngaan รายงาน to report

rák รัก to love

rák laeh ao-cai sài รักและเอาใจใส่ to care for, love

ráksǎa รักษา to treat (medically)

ráksǎa khwaam láp รักษาความลับ to keep a secret

ràksǎa láeo รักษาแล้ว recovered, cured

ramkhaan รำคาญ annoyed

rán รั้น stubborn, headstrong

rang รัง nest

rangkìat รังเกียจ to mind, be displeased

rao เรา we, us

rao rao ราวๆ around (approximately)

ráp รับ to receive; to pick someone up

ráp chái รับใช้ to serve

ráp ngoen duean รับเงินเดือน to collect payment

ráp phìt châwp รับผิดชอบ to be responsible

ráp thohrasàp รับโทรศัพท์ answer the phone

ráprawng รับรอง to guarantee

rátthabaan รัฐบาล government

R

raw รอ to wait for; see also **khawi**

ráwi ร้อย hundred

rawi phîean รอยเปื้อน stain

ráwn ร้อน hot (temperature)

ráwng hâi ร้องไห้ to cry, weep

ráwng phlehng ร้องเพลง to sing

rawng tháo รองเท้า shoes

rawng tháo tàe รองเท้าแตะ sandals, slippers

râwp รอบ circuit, trip, 12-year cycle

râwt chiiwít รอดชีวิต to survive

rawàang ระหว่าง during, between, among, while

rawang ระวัง careful!, look out!, to be cautious

râwp râwp รอบๆ around (surrounding)

ra-yá wehlaa ระยะเวลา period (of time)

rêng dùan เร่งด่วน urgent

reo เร็ว fast, rapid, quick

reo kwàa pòkkatì เร็วกว่าปกติ early

reo reo เร็วๆ hurry up!

rîak เรียก call, summon

rîak ráwng เรียกร้อง to urge, push for, demand

rian เรียน to learn, study

rĭan เหรียญ coin, dollar

riang khwaam เรียงความ essay

rîap เรียบ even (smooth), flat, level; plain (not fancy)

rîap ráwi เรียบร้อย neat, orderly, tidy

rîip รีบ to hurry

rîit sûea รีดเสื้อ to iron (clothing)

rim ริม edge

rim fàng mâeh náam ริมฝั่งแม่น้ำ bank (of river)

rim fĭi pàak ริมฝีปาก lips

rín ริน to pour

ripbîn ริบบิ้น ribbon

rôehm เริ่ม to begin, start

rôhk โรค disease

rohng โรง godown, structure, large shed

rohng lákhawn โรงละคร theater (drama)

rohng năng โรงหนัง cinema, movie house

rohng ngaan โรงงาน factory

rohng phayaabaan โรงพยาบาล hospital

rohng rót โรงรถ garage (for parking)

rohngraehm โรงแรม hotel

rohngrian โรงเรียน school

rók รก in a mess

rôm ร่ม umbrella

rôm ngao ร่มเงา shade

rópkuan รบกวน to bother, disturb

rót รถ car, automobile, vehicle

rót รส taste

rót banthúk รถบรรทุก truck

rót cakrayaan รถจักรยาน bicycle

rót fai รถไฟ train

rót khěn รถเข็น cart (pushcart)

rót meh รถเมล์ bus

rót meh lék รถเมล์เล็ก minibus

rót tháeksîi รถแท็กซี่ taxi

rót túk túk รถตุ๊กตุ๊ก tuktuk taxi

rót yon รถยนต์ automobile, car

rúa รั้ว fence

ruai รวย rich, well off, wealthy

ruam รวม to add, include

rûam phêht ร่วมเพศ to have sex, sexual activity

ruam tháng รวมทั้ง included, including

rûap ruam รวบรวม to assemble, gather

ruea เรือ boat, ship

rûea รั่ว to leak

ruea khâam fâak เรือข้ามฟาก ferry

ruean เรือน outhouse, building

ruean ráprawng khàehk เรือนรับรอง แขก guesthouse

rûeang เรื่อง matter, issue, story

rûeang mâak เรื่องมาก fussy

rúeduu ฤดู season

rúeduu bai mái phlì ฤดูใบไม้ผลิ spring (season)

rúeduu bai mái rûang ฤดูใบไม้ร่วง autumn, fall

rúeduu fǒn ฤดูฝน rainy season

rúeduu nǎo ฤดูหนาว cool season, winter

rúeduu ráwn ฤดูร้อน hot season, summer

rǔeh หรือ *end particle*: question word asks for confirmation (perhaps with some doubt or surprise)

rǔeh, rúe หรือ or

rǔeh mâi kâw... หรือไม่ก็... or else

rûn รุ่น model (type); 'class' of people

run raehng รุนแรง severe

ruu รู hole

rúu รู้ to know, realize, be aware of

rǔu rǎa หรูหรา luxurious

ruu camùuk รูจมูก nostril

rúu sǎmnúek รู้สำนึก to be conscious of

rúucàk รู้จัก to know a person, be acquainted with

rûup รูป shape, picture

rûup khài รูปไข่ oval (shape)

rûup pân รูปปั้น sculpture, statue

rûup phâap รูปภาพ picture

rûup râang รูปร่าง form (shape), appearance

rûup thài รูปถ่าย photograph

rûup wâat รูปวาด drawing

rúusùek รู้สึก to feel

rúusùek phìt รู้สึกผิด to feel guilty

S

sà wâi náam สระว่ายน้ำ swimming pool

sǎahàt สาหัส severe, serious, grave

sǎahèht สาเหตุ source

sâak pràk hàk phang ซากปรักหักพัง remains (historical)

sǎakhǎa สาขา branch

sǎam สาม three

sǎam lìam สามเหลี่ยม triangle

sǎam sìp สามสิบ thirty

sǎamâat สามารถ can, be able to, be capable of

sǎamâat mii dâi สามารถมีได้ to afford

sǎamii สามี husband

sǎan câo ศาลเจ้า temple (Chinese)

sâang สร้าง to build, create

sâang khwaam pratháp cai สร้างความประทับใจ to make an impression

sâap ทราบ to know (polite)

sâap súeng ซาบซึ้ง grateful

sàatsanǎa ศาสนา religion

sàatsanǎa khrít ศาสนาคริสต์ Christianity

sàatsanǎa phút ศาสนาพุทธ Buddhism

sà-àat สะอาด clean

sabai สบาย comfortable

sabai dii lǒeh สบายดีหรือ how are you?

sabùu สบู่ soap

sadaehng แสดง to display, show; to express (opinion)

sadùak สะดวก convenient

sàdueh สะดือ stomach, belly

sǎehn แสน hundred thousand

sǎehng aathít แสงอาทิตย์ sunlight

sàehp แสบ to sting, smart

sahàrâatchà-anaacàk, yuu kheh สหราชอาณาจักร, ยูเค United Kingdom

sahàrát amehríkaa สหรัฐอเมริกา United States

sai ทราย sand

sài ใส่ to wear, put on

sái ซ้าย left (direction)

sǎi สาย late; *classifier* for connecting things eg. roads, routes and telephone lines

sǎi mâi wâang สายไม่ว่าง busy line, engaged (telephone)

sái mueh ซ้ายมือ left-hand side

S

sài phaw dii ใส่พอดี to fit

sák สัก about, at least, merely

sák hàeng สักแห่ง somewhere

sák khráng สักครั้ง just this once

sák khrûu สักครู่ just a moment

sák phák สักพัก for a while

sakàwtlaehn สก็อตแลนด์ Scotland

sakòt สะกด to spell

sàksɨ̌i ศักดิ์ศรี pride

sàksìt ศักดิ์สิทธิ์ holy, sacred

salàk สลัก to engrave

salàp สลับ to alternate

salìp สลิป slip (petticoat, underskirt)

samaachík สมาชิก member

samǎi kàwn สมัยก่อน those days, olden times

samǎi mài สมัยใหม่ these days, modern times

samǎi níi สมัยนี้ nowadays

samǎwng สมอง mind, brain

samǐan เสมียน clerk

sǎmlii สำลี cotton wool

sǎmnao สำเนา photocopy, copy

samǒeh เสมอ always

sǎmphaará สัมภาระ belongings

sǎmphâat สัมภาษณ์ interview

sǎmphanthá́wong สัมพันธวงศ์ Samphanthawong, area 2 1/2 km SSE of Bangkok center

sǎmràp สำหรับ intended for, for

sǎmrawng สำรอง to reserve (ask for in advance)

sǎmrèt สำเร็จ to succeed, fulfill; complete (finished)

samùt สมุด notebook, exercise book

samùt dai-aarîi สมุดไดอารี่ diary, daybook

sàn สั่น to shake, vibrate, tremble

sân สั้น brief, short (concise)

sanǎam สนาม field, empty space

sanǎam bin สนามบิน airport

sanǎam yâa สนามหญ้า courtyard

sǎnchâat สัญชาติ nationality

sàng สั่ง to order, command; to order something

sǎngkèht สังเกต to notice

sangòp สงบ peaceful, calm

sanǒeh เสนอ to bring up (topic), propose (a matter) present; to offer, suggest

sǎntiphâap สันติภาพ peace

sanùk สนุก fun, enjoyable

sǎnyaa สัญญา to promise

sǎnyalák สัญลักษณ์ sign, symbol

sâo เศร้า sad, sorrowful, sorrow

sǎo สาว girl, young woman

sǎo เสา post, column

sǎo aathít เสาร์อาทิตย์ weekend

sà-oht sà-awng สะโอดสะอง slender

sáp sáwn ซับซ้อน complicated

sàp sǒn สับสน to confuse

sàpdaa nâa สัปดาห์หน้า next week

sàpdaa สัปดาห์ week; see also **aathít**

saphaan สะพาน bridge

saphâap สภาพ condition (status)

saphái สะไภ้ female in-law

sapparót สับปะรด pineapple

sapring สปริง spring (metal part)

sà-sǒm สะสม to store

sàt สัตว์ animal

sàt líang สัตว์เลี้ยง pet animal

sataang, stang สตางค์ Thai money

satǎapàtyákam สถาปัตยกรรม architecture

satáat สตาร์ท to start a car

sataehm แสตมป์ stamp (postage)

sathǎan thîi สถานที่ place

sathǎan thûut สถานทูต embassy

sathǎanakaan สถานการณ์ situation, how things are

sathǎanii สถานี station

sathǎanii rót fay สถานีรถไฟ train station

sathǎanii rót fay hǔa lamphohng สถานีรถไฟหัวลำโพง Hualampong, Bangkok's main railway station

sathǎanii rót meh สถานีรถเมล์ bus station
satháwn สะท้อน to reflect
sàtruu ศัตรู enemy
sattàwát ศตวรรษ century
satuun สตูล stool
sawàang สว่าง bright, brilliant (light)
sa-wàt dii สวัสดี hello, hi
sawi ซอย alley, lane, soi
sâwi สร้อย bracelet
sâwi khaw สร้อยคอ necklace
sawít สวิทช์ switch
sâwm ซ่อม to mend, repair
sâwm ส้อม fork (for spoon)
sǎwn สอน to teach
sâwn yùu ซ่อนอยู่ hidden
sawng ซอง envelope
sǎwng สอง two
sǎwng sǎam สองสาม a few
sǎwng thâo สองเท่า double
sàwp สอบ to examine
sàwp phàan สอบผ่าน to pass a test/exam
sáws ซอส sauce
sáws phrík, sáwt phrík ซอสพริก chili sauce
sèht nùeng sùan sìi เศษหนึ่งส่วนสี่ (1/4) quarter
sèht sataang, sèht stang เศษสตางค์ small change
sèhthakìt เศรษฐกิจ economy
sen เซ็น to sign
sen เซ็นต์ centimeter
sên เส้น line (mark); *classifier* for string-like things eg. noodles, hair
sên tháyaehng mum เส้นทะแยงมุม diagonal
sèt เสร็จ to finish
sèt láeo เสร็จแล้ว done, finished, completed
sèt sîn เสร็จสิ้น to end
sí ซิ *end particle*: gives a mild order by the speaker

sî ซิ *end particle*: gives a stronger order by the speaker
sǐa เสีย broken (machine), out of order, spoiled; off (food), gone bad
sǐa cai เสียใจ to feel sorry, regretful
sǐa nhoen เสียเงิน to lose money
sǐa salà เสียสละ to sacrifice, give up one's place
sǐang เสียง sound, noise, voice
sǐang dang เสียงดัง noisy, loud
sǐang thaang mehl เสียงทางเมล์ voicemail
sìi สี่ four
sǐi สี color, paint
sǐi chomphuu สีชมพู pink
sii dii ซีดี CD
sii dii rawm ซีดีรอม CD-ROM
sǐi fáa สีฟ้า blue
sìi lìam สี่เหลี่ยม square (shape)
sìi lìam phúehn phâa สี่เหลี่ยมพื้นผ้า rectangle
sìi sìp สี่สิบ forty
sǐi sôm สีส้ม orange (color)
sǐi thao สีเทา gray
sǐi tòk สีตก color runs
sii-íu ซีอิ๊ว soy sauce (salty)
sii-íu wǎan ซีอิ๊วหวาน soy sauce (sweet)
siikaa ซิการ์ cigar
sìiyâehk สี่แยก intersection
sìng สิ่ง item, individual thing
sìng khǎwng สิ่งของ object, thing
sìng kìt khwǎang สิ่งกีดขวาง hindrance
sìng wâeht láwm สิ่งแวดล้อม the environment, surroundings
sǐnghǎakhom สิงหาคม August
sǐngkhápoh สิงคโปร์ Singapore
sǐnlabin ศิลปิน artist
sǐnlapà ศิลปะ art
sìp สิบ ten
sìp cèt สิบเจ็ด seventeen
sìp èt สิบเอ็ด eleven
sìp hâa สิบห้า fifteen

S

sìp hòk สิบหก sixteen

sìp kâo สิบเก้า nineteen

sìp pàeht สิบแปด eighteen

sìp sǎam สิบสาม thirteen

sìp sǎwng สิบสอง twelve

sìp sìi สิบสี่ fourteen

sìtthí สิทธิ rights

sòehf เซริฟ serve

sohfǎa โซฟา couch, sofa

sòht โสด single (not married)

sòkkapròk สกปรก dirty

sôm ส้ม orange (citrus fruit)

sôm hèht phǒn สมเหตุผล reasonable, sensible

sôm oh ส้มโอ pomelo

sǒmbàt สมบัติ possessions, property

sǒmbuun สมบูรณ์ to be whole, entire, complete, healthy

sǒmmút สมมุติ to suppose

son ซน naughty

sǒncai สนใจ interested in

sòng ส่ง to deliver, mail, send

sòng àwk ส่งออก to export

sòng fáek(s) ส่งแฟกซ์ to fax

sòng iimeh(l) ส่งอีเมล์ to email

sǒngkhraam สงคราม war

sǒngsǎi สงสัย to doubt, suspect

sòt สด fresh

suai ซวย bad luck

sûam ส้วม toilet

sùan ส่วน part (not whole)

sǔan สวน garden, yard

sùan nùeng ส่วนหนึ่ง partly

sǔan sǎathaaraná สวนสาธารณะ gardens, park

sǔan sàt สวนสัตว์ zoo

sùan tua ส่วนตัว private

sùan yài ส่วนใหญ่ mostly

sùat mon สวดมนต์ to pray

sǔay สวย pretty (of places, things), beautiful

sûea เสื้อ blouse

sùea เสื่อ mat

sǔea เสือ tiger

sûea chán nai เสื้อชั้นใน undershirt

sûea chóeht เสื้อเชิ้ต shirt

sûea kan nǎo เสื้อกันหนาว windcheater, zipped jacket

sûea khlum เสื้อคลุม dressing gown

sûea khlum àap náam เสื้อคลุมอาบน้ำ bathrobe

sûea klâam เสื้อกล้าม briefs

sûea nâwk เสื้อนอก coat, overcoat

sûea nawn เสื้อนอน pyjamas

sûea phâa เสื้อผ้า clothes, clothing, garments

sûea yûeht เสื้อยืด vest, undershirt, teeshirt

súeh ซื้อ to buy

sûehsàt ซื่อสัตย์ to be honest

sùeksǎa ศึกษา to educate

sùk สุก cooked, well-cooked; ripe

sùk láeo สุกแล้ว done (cooked)

sùksǎn wan kòeht สุขสันต์วันเกิด happy birthday!

sùksǎn wan pii mài สุขสันต์วันปีใหม่ happy new year!

súp kâwn ซุปก้อน soup (chunky)

sùphâap สุภาพ to be polite

sùphâap satrii สุภาพสตรี lady

súpôehmaakèt ซุปเปอร์มาเก็ต supermarket

surào สุเหร่า mosque; Indian temple

sùt khùa สุดขั้ว extremely

sùt sàpdaa สุดสัปดาห์ weekend

sùt thái สุดท้าย final, last

sùu สู่ to, toward (a person); into see also nai

sûu สู้ to fight (physically)

sûu róp สู้รบ battle

sǔun ศูนย์ zero

sǔun klaang ศูนย์กลาง middle, center, central

sǔung สูง high, tall

sùup สูบ to pump, to smoke (habit)

sùut สูท suit (clothes)

sùut aahǎan สูตรอาหาร recipe

T

taa ตา grandfather (maternal); eye

taa bàwt ตาบอด blind

taa châng ตาชั่ง scales

tàak hâehng ตากแห้ง dry out (in the sun)

taakhài ตาข่าย net

taam ตาม to follow along

taam kòtmǎi ตามกฎหมาย legal, according to law

taam lamdàp ตามลำดับ sequence, order

taam lǎng ตามหลัง to follow behind

taam pokkatì ตามปกติ usually

taam thîi ตามที่.... according to

tàang ต่าง to differ

tàang prathêht ต่างประเทศ foreign, overseas, abroad

tàang tàang ต่างๆ various

taaraang wehlaa ตารางเวลา timetable

tàe และ to touch

tàeh แต่ but

tàeh lá แต่ละ each, every

tàehk แตก broken, shattered, cracked

tàehk la-ìat แตกละเอียด break, shatter into pieces

tàehk yâehk แตกแยก to break apart

taehng แตง melon

tàehng, khǐan แต่ง, เขียน compose, write (letters, books, music)

taehng kwaa แตงกวา cucumber

taehng moh แตงโม watermelon

tàehng ngaan แต่งงาน to marry, get married

tàehng ngaan láeo แต่งงานแล้ว married

tàehng tua แต่งตัว to get dressed

tai ตาย to die, dead

tai ไต kidney

tài ได่ to go up, climb (hills, mountains)

tâi ใต้ under; south

tâifùn ได้ฝุ่น typhoon

takhǎw ตะขอ hook

takhrái ตะไคร้ lemongrass

takiang ตะเกียง lamp

takìap ตะเกียบ chopsticks

takohn ตะโกน to cry out, shout, yell

tàkrâa ตะกร้า basket

talàat ตลาด market

talàwt ตลอด all the time

talàwt chiiwít ตลอดชีวิต lifetime

talàwt pai ตลอดไป for ever

talìngchan ตลิ่งชัน Talingchan, area on the west bank 6^1/$_2$ km WNW of Bangkok center

talòk ตลก funny

tàm ต่ำ low

tamnaan ตำนาน legend

tamnàeng ตำแหน่ง position

tamruàt ตำรวจ police

tâng tôn ตั้งต้น start, beginning

tâng yùu ตั้งอยู่ to be situated, located

tângcai ตั้งใจ to intend, pay attention

tângtàeh ตั้งแต่ since

tao เตา cooker, stove

tâo hûu เต้าหู้ beancurd, tofu

tào naa เต่านา turtle (land)

tao òp เตาอบ oven

tào tanù เต่าตนุ turtle (sea)

tàp ตับ liver

tapuu ตะปู nail (spike)

tàt ตัด to cut

tàt phǒm ตัดผม to have a haircut

tàtsǐn cai ตัดสินใจ to decide

tàw ต่อ extension (telephone)

tàw pai ต่อไป next (in line, sequence)

tàw rawng ต่อรอง to bargain

tàw tâan ต่อต้าน to oppose

tawan àwk ตะวันออก east

tawan àwk chǐang nǔea
ตะวันออกเฉียงเหนือ north-east

tawan àwk chǐang tâi
ตะวันออกเฉียงใต้ south-east

tawan tòk ตะวันตก west

tawan tòk chǐang nǔea ตะวันตกเฉียง เหนือ north west

tawan tòk chǐang tâi ตะวันตกเฉียงใต้ south-west

tawn ตอน piece, portion, section

tawn klaang khuehn ตอนกลางคืน at night

tâwn ráp ต้อนรับ to welcome

tawn rôehm tôn ตอนเริ่มต้น beginning

tawn thîang ตอนเที่ยง noon

tawn yen ตอนเย็น evening

tâwng ต้อง have to, must

tâwng hâam ต้องห้าม forbidden

tâwngkaan ต้องการ to need, want

tàwp ตอบ to answer, respond; reply, response

tàwp klàp ตอบกลับ to reply (in speech)

tàwp sanǎwng ตอบสนอง to respond, react

tàwp sanǎwng tàw... ตอบสนองต่อ ... to react to

tem เต็ม full

tên ram เต้นรำ to dance, disco

thâa ถ้า if

thâa ruea ท่าเรือ harbor, port; wharf, pier

thaa sǐi ทาสี to paint (house, furniture)

thâa thaang ท่าทาง appearance, looks, gesture

tháa thai ท้าทาย challenge

thǎam ถาม to enquire

thǎam kìao kàp ถามเกี่ยวกับ to ask about

thǎan ฐาน base, foundation, basis

thaan ทาน to eat; see also **kin**

thaan aahǎan yen ทานอาหารเย็น to eat dinner

thaan khâo thîang ทานข้าวเที่ยง to eat lunch

thǎaná ฐานะ status, station in life

thaang ทาง way, path, direction

thaang àwk ทางออก exit, way out

thaang doehn nai tùek ทางเดินในตึก corridor

thaang kaan phâeht ทางการแพทย์ medical

thaang khâo ทางเข้า entrance, way in

thaang lûeak ทางเลือก choice

thaang rótfai ทางรถไฟ railroad, railway

thaarók ทารก baby

thàat ถาด tray

thǎawawn ถาวร permanent

thaayâat ทายาท descendant

thaehn แทน to replace

thaehn thîi แทนที่ instead of

thaehn thîi ca... แทนที่จะ... rather than

thaehng แทง pierce, penetrate

thâehp ca mâi แทบจะไม่ hardly, barely

tháeksîi แท็กซี่ taxi

thǎeo níi แถวนี้ around (nearby)

thahǎan ทหาร soldier

thahǎan aakàat ทหารอากาศ airman, airwoman; air force

thahǎan bòk ทหารบก army soldier; army

thahǎan ruea ทหารเรือ sailor; navy

thai ไทย Thai

thài ถ่าย to defecate

thài rûup ถ่ายรูป to photograph

thài sǎmnao ถ่ายสำเนา to photocopy

thák thai ทักทาย to greet; to say hello

thaláw ทะเลาะ argument

thaleh ทะเล sea

thaleh sàap ทะเลสาบ lake

thaleh sai ทะเลทราย desert (arid land)

tham ทำ do, perform an action, make, act, undergo

thâm ถ้ำ cave

tham aahǎan ทำอาหาร to cook

T

tham dii thîi sùt ทำดีที่สุด
do one's best

tham dûai mái ทำด้วยไม้ wooden

tham hǎi ทำหาย to lose, mislay

tham hâi cèp ทำให้เจ็บ
to hurt (cause pain)

tham hâi com náam ทำให้จมน้ำ
to drown

tham hâi chamrút ทำให้ชำรุด
to damage

tham hâi hâehng ทำให้แห้ง to dry

tham hâi lâa cháa ทำให้ล่าช้า delay

tham hâi mâi phaw cai
ทำให้ไม่พอใจ offend

tham hâi pen rûup ทำให้เป็นรูป
to form shape

tham hâi pháeh ทำให้แพ้ to defeat

tham hâi phráwm ทำให้พร้อม
to make ready

tham hâi pùat ทำให้ปวด to ache

tham hâi ráwn ทำให้ร้อน to heat

tham hâi sèt ทำให้เสร็จ to complete,
finish off

tham hâi yen ทำให้เย็น to cool

tham khwaam sa-àat ทำความสะอาด
to clean

tham lai ทำลาย to destroy

tham ngaan ทำงาน to function, work

tham phìt ทำผิด wrong (morally)

tham sám ทำซ้ำ to repeat

tham sǒngkhraam ทำสงคราม
to make war

tham tàw pai ทำต่อไป to continue on

tham tàwp ทำตอบ to reply (in deeds)

tham tua dii ทำตัวดี well-behaved

tham tua hâi sanùk ทำตัวให้สนุก
to enjoy oneself

tham wícai ทำวิจัย to research

thammachâat ธรรมชาติ nature

thammadaa ธรรมดา common,
frequent, simple, normal

thammai ทำไม why?

thammaniam ธรรมเนียม custom,
tradition

than ทัน to catch, make it on time

thân ท่าน sir (term of address)

than samǎi ทันสมัย modern

than thii ทันที at once, immediately,
suddenly

thanaakhaan ธนาคาร bank (finance)

thanai ทนาย lawyer

thanǎwm ถนอม reserve (for animals)

thanǎwm aahǎan ถนอมอาหาร cured,
preserved (foods)

tháng khûu ทั้งคู่ both

tháng...láe... ทั้ง...และ... both...and

tháng...láe...mâi... ทั้ง...และ...ไม่...
neither...nor...

tháng mòt ทั้งหมด entirety, whole,
total, in total, altogether, all

thanǒn ถนน road, street

thanwaakhom ธันวาคม December

tháo เท้า foot

thâo nán เท่านั้น just, only

thâo thiam เท่าเทียม equal

thâorai เท่าไร how much?

tháphii ทัพพี dipper, ladle

thàt pai ถัดไป next to

thátsanákhatì ทัศนคติ attitude

thaw ทอ to weave

thawǎan nàk ทวารหนัก anus

tháwffîi, tháwpfîi ท็อฟฟี่ candy,
sweets

thǎwi lang ถอยหลัง backward,
to reverse, back up

thǎwi pai ถอยไป to back up

tháwîip ทวีป continent

thawng ทอง gold

tháwng ท้อง pregnant

thawng daehng ทองแดง copper

thawng sǎmrít ทองสัมฤทธิ์ bronze

thàwt ถอด take off (clothes)

thâwt ทอด to fry, fried

thá-yaehng mum ทะแยงมุม
diagonally

théhp เทป adhesive tape; cassette

théhp widiioh เทปวิดีโอ
video cassette

thêhtsakaan เทศกาล festival

thennís, thennít เท็นนิส tennis

thiam เทียม false (imitation), artificial

thian เทียน candle

thîang เถียง to argue

thîang khuehn เที่ยงคืน midnight

thîang wan เที่ยงวัน midday

thîao bin เที่ยวบิน flight

thii ที time, occasion;
  classifier for times

thîi ที่ in, at (space); place, space;
  that, which, the one who; portion,
  serve (food)

thîi bâan ที่บ้าน at home

thîi cing ที่จริง actually, in fact

thîi kìao khâwng ที่เกี่ยวข้อง involved

thîi kwâang ที่กว้าง spacious

thii la nít ทีละนิด gradually

thîi láeo ที่แล้ว ago

thii lǎng ทีหลัง later

thîi lǔea ที่เหลือ left, leftover,
  remaining, the rest

thîi nǎi ที่ไหน where?

thîi nǎi kâw dâi ที่ไหนก็ได้ anywhere

thîi nân ที่นั่น there

thîi nâng ที่นั่ง seat

thîi nawn ที่นอน mattress

thîi nîi ที่นี่ here

thîi nôhn ที่โน่น over there

thîi pám ที่ปั๊ม stamp (ink)

thîi phák ที่พัก accommodation

thîi râap ที่ราบ plain (level ground)

thîi rawng caan ที่รองจาน tablemat

thîi sǎam ...ที่สาม third...

thîi sǎathaaraná ที่สาธารณะ public
  place

thîi sǎmkhan ที่สำคัญ mainly

thîi sǎwng ...ที่สอง second...

thîi sìap plák ที่เสียบปลั๊ก socket
  (electric)

thîi sùt ที่สุด most (superlative)

thîi tham ngaan ที่ทำงาน office

thîi thǔeh ที่ถือ handle

thîi wâang ที่ว่าง room, space

thii wii ทีวี TV

thii wii, thohrathát ทีวี, โทรทัศน์
  television

thîi yùu ที่อยู่ address

thîi yùu iimeh(l) ที่อยู่อีเมล์
  email address

thiim, khaná ทีม, คณะ team

thíng ทิ้ง to desert, abandon;
  to throw away

thíng wái ทิ้งไว้
  leave behind on purpose

thíp ทิป tip (gratuity)

thoeh เธอ you (intimate)

thoehm เทอม school term

thohrasàp โทรศัพท์ telephone

thohrasàp mueh thǔeh โทรศัพท์มือถือ
  mobile phone

thôht โทษ to blame

thòk panhǎa ถกปัญหา to discuss

thon thúk ทนทุกข์ to suffer

thon thúk càak... ทนทุกข์จาก...
  to suffer from

thonabàt ธนบัตร note (currency)

thonburii ธนบุรี Thonburi, area on
  the west bank, 7 km WSW of
  Bangkok center; capital before
  Bangkok (Krungthep)

thong ธง flag

thót lawng ทดลอง to test

thùa ถั่ว beans, peas

thùa daehng ถั่วแดง kidney beans

thùa dam ถั่วดำ black beans

thùa fàk yao ถั่วฝักยาว green beans

thùa lísǒng ถั่วลิสง peanuts

thùa ngâwk ถั่วงอก
  mung bean sprouts

thûa pai ทั่วไป general, all-purpose

thùa wǎan ถั่วหวาน snowpeas

thûai ถ้วย cup

thǔeh ถือ to hold something;
  to have a belief

thǔeng ถึง to attain, reach, get to

thǔeng máeh wâa... ถึงแม้ว่า...
  although

thúk ทุก every
thúk chanít ทุกชนิด every kind of
thúk khon ทุกคน everybody, everyone
thúk khuehn ทุกคืน nightly
thúk sìng ทุกสิ่ง everything
thúk thii ทุกที every time
thúk thîi ทุกที่ everywhere
thun ทุน funds, funding
thǔng ถุง bag
thǔng mueh ถุงมือ gloves
thǔng tháo ถุงเท้า socks
thǔng yaang (anaamai) ถุงยาง (อนามัย) condom
thurá ธุระ errand, business matter, to attend to
thurákìt ธุรกิจ trade, business
thurian ทุเรียน durian
thǔu ถู to scrub
thùuk ถูก cheap; to be right, correct; *passive* form (acted on by...)
thùuk luehm ถูกลืม forgotten
thùuk taam cai ถูกตามใจ spoiled (does not work)
thùuk tâwng ถูกต้อง correct
thùuk tham lai ถูกทำลาย destroyed, ruined
thûup ธูป incense
thûut ทูต ambassador
tîa เตี้ย short (not tall)
tiang เตียง bed
tii ตี hit, strike, beat
tii khâa ตีค่า to value
tìt ติด stuck, won't move
tìt kan ติดกัน close together, tight
tìt kàp ติดกับ to be attached to, stuck to
tìt tàw ติดต่อ contact, get in touch with
tìt tàw kan ติดต่อกัน to connect together
tó โต๊ะ desk, table
toehm เติม to fill

toh โต grow, be growing (plant), grow up (child); grown up, mature, big
toh khûen โตขึ้น to grow larger
tôh tàwp โต้ตอบ to reply to, answer to
tòk ตก to fall
tòk cai ตกใจ alarmed, startled
tòk plaa ตกปลา to fish
tòklong ตกลง agreed!, okay
tòklong tham ตกลงทำ to agree to do something
tôm ต้ม to boil
tôm yam ต้มยำ soup (spicy stew)
tôn mái ต้นไม้ plant, tree
tòp tàeng ตบแต่ง to decorate
trày trawng ไตร่ตรอง to think, ponder, consider
triam เตรียม prepare, make ready
triam phráwm เตรียมพร้อม prepared, ready
triam tua เตรียมตัว to get ready
trong ตรง direct, non-stop; straight (not crooked)
trong khâam ตรงข้าม opposite (contrary)
trong khâam kàp ตรงข้ามกับ across from
trong klaang ตรงกลาง center, middle
trong pai khâng nâa ตรงไปข้างหน้า straight ahead
trong wehlaa ตรงเวลา on time, punctual
trùat ตรวจ to inspect
trùat sàwp ตรวจสอบ to check, verify, test
tua ตัว body, *classifier* for animals, tables, chairs and clothes
tǔa ตั๋ว ticket (for transport, entertainment)
tua aksǎwn ตัวอักษร character (written)
tua cing ตัวจริง original
tua chiipakhǎo ตัวชีปะขาว moth

tua lêhk ตัวเลข figure, number

tŭa pai klàp ตั๋วไปกลับ return ticket

tŭa thîao diao ตั๋วเที่ยวเดียว one-way
ticket

tua yàang ตัวอย่าง example, sample

tua yàang chên ตัวอย่างเช่น such as,
for example

tuean เตือน to remind, warn

tûehn ตื้น shallow

tùehn ตื่น wake

tùehn khûen ตื่นขึ้น awake, wake up

tùehn tên ตื่นเต้น to be excited

tulaakhom ตุลาคม October

tûm hŭu ตุ้มหู earrings

tûu ตู้ cupboard

tûu hâi khâwmuun ตู้ให้ข้อมูล
information booth

tûu thohrasàp ตู้โทรศัพท์
telephone box

tûu yaam tamrùat ตู้ยามตำรวจ
police box

tûu yen ตู้เย็น refrigerator

U

ûak อ้วก to be sick, vomit

ûan อ้วน to be fat, plump

ùbatìhèht อุบัติเหตุ accident

udom อุดม fertile

ùe อี to defecate (colloq.); see also
khîi

ùehn อื่น different, other

ùn อุ่น to warm

unhàphuum อุณหภูมิ temperature

ùtcaará อุจาระ feces

ùtsăahàkam อุตสาหกรรม industry

ùu sôm rót อู่ซ่อมรถ garage (for
repairs)

W

wâa... ว่า...
that (introducing a quotation)

wăan หวาน sweet

waang วาง place, put

wâang ว่าง free, unoccupied

wâang ngaan ว่างงาน unemployed

waang phăehn วางแผน to plan

wâang plào ว่างเปล่า empty

waarasăan วารสาร magazine

wâat วาด to draw

wâat phâap วาดภาพ to imagine

wáe แวะ to stop by, pay a visit

wăehn แหวน ring (jewelry)

wâen săi taa แว่นสายตา eyeglasses,
spectacles

wâen taa แว่นตา glasses, spectacles

wái ไว้ to keep, preserve

wái cai ไว้ใจ to trust

wâi náam ว่ายน้ำ to bathe, swim

wai rûn วัยรุ่น teenager

wai(n) ไวน์ wine

wan วัน day of the week

wan aathít วันอาทิตย์ Sunday

wan angkhaan วันอังคาร Tuesday

wan can วันจันทร์ Monday

wan duean pii kòeht วันเดือนปีเกิด
date of birth

wan kòeht วันเกิด birthday

wan níi วันนี้ today

wan phárúehàt (sabawdii) วัน
พฤหัสบดี Thursday

wan phút วันพุธ Wednesday

wan săo วันเสาร์ Saturday

wan sùk วันศุกร์ Friday

wan thîi... วันที่... date (of the
month), on (date)

wan wén wan วันเว้นวัน
every other day

wan yùt วันหยุด day off

wan yùt phák phàwn วันหยุดพักผ่อน
holiday, vacation

wan yùt râatchakaan วันหยุดราชการ
public holiday

wan yùt thêhtsakaan วันหยุดเทศกาล
festival holiday

wang วัง palace

wăng หวัง to hope

wannákhadii วรรณคดี literature

Y

wâo ว่าว kite

wàt หวัด cold

wát วัด to measure; temple (Thai, Hindu-Balinese)

wát booraan วัดโบราณ temple (ancient)

wát phrá kâeo วัดพระแก้ว Temple of the Emerald Buddha

wàt yài หวัดใหญ่ flu

wátsadù วัสดุ material, ingredient

wattanátham วัฒนธรรม culture

wáwis-mehl วอยซ์เมล์ voicemail

wehl(s) เวลส์ Wales

wehlaa เวลา when, at the time; time

wén เว้น to skip, excepting

wép sáit เว็บไซต์ website

wîatnaam เวียดนาม Vietnam

wíchaa วิชา subject of study

wîi หวี comb

wiisâa วีซ่า visa

wiisiiaa วีซีอาร์ VCR

wínaathii วินาที second

wîng วิ่ง to run

wîng nǐi วิ่งหนี run away

wíthayaalai วิทยาลัย college

wíthayaasàat วิทยาศาสตร์ science

wítthayú วิทยุ radio

wíthii วิธี way, method

wiu วิว scenery, view, panorama

wóht โหวต to vote

wong klom วงกลม circle

wua วัว cow

wûn wai วุ่นวาย busy (crowded)

Y

yaa ยา drug, medicine, pills

yàa หย่า to divorce

yàa อย่า don't!

yâa ย่า grandmother (paternal)

yâa หญ้า grass

yaa bâa ยาบ้า drug (recreational), amphetamines

yàa láeo หย่าแล้ว divorced

yaa mét ยาเม็ด tablets

yaa phít ยาพิษ poison

yaa ráksǎa ยารักษา cure (medical)

yaa sà phǒm ยาสระผม shampoo

yaa sǐi fan ยาสีฟัน toothpaste

yàak อยาก to want

yâak ยาก hard, difficult

yàak dâi อยากได้ would like to get

yaam ยาม time, era; watchman

yaam dùek ยามดึก late at night

yaam kháp khân ยามคับขัน time of emergency

yaan naawaa ยานนาวา Yannawa, area 8 km south of Bangkok center

yaan yon ยานยนต์ motor vehicle

yaang ยาง rubber (substance)

yàang ย่าง roast, grill

yàang อย่าง type, sort, variety, *classifier* for things

yàang hěn dâi chát อย่างเห็นได้ชัด apparently

yàang nák อย่างน้อย least: at least

yàang prayàt อย่างประหยัด economical

yàang reo อย่างเร็ว quickly

yàang sǒmbuun อย่างสมบูรณ์ completely

yàangrai อย่างไร how?

yàangrai kâw taam อย่างไรก็ตาม however

yàap khai หยาบคาย rude

yâat ญาติ relatives (family)

yâeh แย่ terrible

yâeh long แย่ลง worse

yâeh thîi sùt แย่ที่สุด worst

yâehk แยก divide, split up

yâehk kan แยกกัน to separate

yaehm แยม jam

yâehng แย่ง to fight over

yai ยาย grandmother (maternal)

yài ใหญ่ big, large; major (important)

yái ย้าย move from one place to another

Y

yai săngkhráw ใยสังเคราะห์ synthetic (thread)

yam ยำ Thai-style salad

yang ยัง still, even now; not yet (as a reply)

yang mii chiiwít yùu ยังมีชีวิตอยู่ alive

yang-ngai ยังไง how?

yao ยาว long (length)

yaw ยอ to flatter

yâw ย่อ to abbreviate

yâw tua ย่อตัว to crouch down, stoop

yawachon เยาวชน youths (young people)

yawm ráp ยอมรับ to admit, confess; to acknowledge, accept

yâwt ยอด summit, peak; top, fabulous

yâwt yîam ยอดเยี่ยม excellent

yen เย็น cold, cool; afternoon (4 pm to dusk)

yép เย็บ to sew

yép pàk thàk ráwi เย็บปักถักร้อย embroidery

yîam เยี่ยม visit

yìap brèhk เหยียบเบรค to brake

yîi sìp ยี่สิบ twenty

yîipùn ญี่ปุ่น Japan

yím ยิ้ม to smile

yindii ยินดี pleased, glad

yindii tâwn ráp ยินดีต้อนรับ welcome!

ying ยิง to shoot

yìng หยิ่ง elegant

yǐng หญิง female

yîng yài ยิ่งใหญ่ grand, great

yóeh yáe เยอะแยะ lots of

yohn โยน to throw

yók ยก raise, lift

yók lôehk ยกเลิก cancel

yók tua yàang ยกตัวอย่าง to raise an example, for example

yók yâwng ยกย่อง to praise

yót ยศ rank (military, police)

yú ยุ to incite, provoke

yùeak เหยือก jug, pitcher

yuehm ยืม to borrow

yuehn ยืน to stand

yûehn àwk maa ยื่นออกมา to stick out

yuehn khûen ยืนขึ้น to stand (up)

yúet taam ยึดตาม based on

yúet thǔeh ยึดถือ to grasp hold; seize

yung ยุง mosquito

yûng ยุ่ง busy (doing something)

yûng yǒehng ยุ่งเหยิง confused (in a mess)

yúròhp ยุโรป Europe

yùt หยุด to stop, halt

yùt ná หยุดนะ stop it!

yùt wái หยุดไว้ hold back

yútìtham ยุติธรรม just, fair

yùu อยู่ to be, exist, live; live (stay in a place)

yùu kàp thîi อยู่กับที่ stay, remain

yùu trong khâam อยู่ตรงข้าม opposite (facing)

English–Thai

A

abdomen châwng tháwng ช่องท้อง
able to sǎamâat สามารถ
about (approximately) pramaan
ประมาณ
about (regarding) kìaw kàp เกี่ยวกับ
above, upstairs khâang bon ข้างบน
abroad tàang prathêht ต่างประเทศ
absent hǎi pai, mâi yùu หายไป,
ไม่อยู่
accept, to yawm ráp ยอมรับ
accident ùbatìhèht อุบัติเหตุ
accidentally, by chance
doi bangoehn โดยบังเอิญ
accommodation thîi phák ที่พัก
accompany, to pai pen phûean
ไปเป็นเพื่อน
according to taam thîi... ตามที่...
accuse, to klào hǎa กล่าวหา
ache pùat ปวด
ache, to tham hâi pùat ทำให้ปวด
acquaintance khwaam khún khoei
ความคุ้นเคย
acquainted, to be khún khoei kàp
คุ้นเคยกับ
across khâam ข้าม
across from trong khâam kàp
ตรงข้ามกับ
act, to tham, patìbàt ทำ, ปฏิบัติ
action kaan kratham การกระทำ
activity kìcakam กิจกรรม
actually thîi cing ที่จริง
add, to phôehm เพิ่ม
address thîi yùu ที่อยู่
admire, to chom ชม
admit, confess yawm ráp ยอมรับ
adult phûu yài ผู้ใหญ่

advance, go forward kâo nâa
ก้าวหน้า
advance money, deposit
ngoen mát cam เงินมัดจำ
advice kham náenam คำแนะนำ
advise, to náenam แนะนำ
aeroplane khrûeang bin เครื่องบิน
affect, to mii phǒn tàw มีผลต่อ...
affection khwaam rák khrâi
ความรักใคร่
afford, to sǎamâat mii dâi
สามารถมีได้
afraid klua กลัว
after lǎng càak หลังจาก
afternoon (midday) bài บ่าย
afternoon (3 pm to dusk) yen เย็น
afterwards, then lǎng càak nán
หลังจากนั้น
again ...ìik ...อีก
age aayú อายุ
ago thîi láeo ที่แล้ว
agree, to hěn dûai เห็นด้วย
agree to do something, to
tòklong tham ตกลงทำ
agreed! tòklong ตกลง
agreement khâw tòklong ข้อตกลง
air aakàat อากาศ
air conditioning ...pràp aakàat
...ปรับอากาศ
airmail mehl aakàat เมล์อากาศ
airplane khrûeang bin เครื่องบิน
airport sanǎam bin สนามบิน
alcohol, liquor lâo เหล้า
alike mǔean เหมือน
alive yang mii chiiwít yùu
ยังมีชีวิตอยู่
all tháng mòt ทั้งหมด
alley, lane sawi ซอย

45

allow, permit anúyâat อนุญาตให้

allowed to dâi ráp anúyâat
ได้รับอนุญาต

almost kùeap เกือบ

alone khon diao คนเดียว

already láeo แล้ว

also dûai ด้วย

although thùeng máeh wâa ถึงแม้ว่า

altogether, in total tháng mòt
ทั้งหมด

always samôeh เสมอ

ambassador thûut ทูต

America amehríkaa อเมริกา

American khon amehríkan
คนอเมริกัน

among rawàang ระหว่าง

amount camnuan จำนวน

ancestor banpháburùt บรรพบุรุษ

ancient bohraan โบราณ

and láe, kàp และ, กับ

anger khwaam kròht ความโกรธ

angry kròht โกรธ

animal sàt สัตว์

ankle khâw tháo ข้อเท้า

annoyed ramkhaan รำคาญ

another (different) ìik... อีก...

another one ìik an nùeng อีกอันหนึ่ง

annual pracam pii ประจำปี

answer, response kham tàwp
คำตอบ

answer, to respond tàwp ตอบ

answer the phone ráp thohrasàp
รับโทรศัพท์

answering machine khrûeang ráp
thohrasàp เครื่องรับโทรศัพท์

antiques khâwng kào ของเก่า

anus thawǎan nàk ทวารหนัก

anybody, anyone khrai kâw dâi
ใครก็ได้

anything arai kâw dâi
อะไรก็ได้

anywhere thîi nǎi kâw dâi ที่ไหนก็ได้

apart nâwk càak นอกจาก

apartment apaatméhn อพาร์ทเมนต์

ape ling ลิง

apologize, to khǎw thôht ขอโทษ

apparently yàang hěn dâi chát
อย่างเห็นได้ชัด

appear, become visible praakòt
ปรากฏ

appearance, looks thâa thaang
ท่าทาง

apple áeppôen แอปเปิล

appliance, electrical khrûeang fai
fáa เครื่องไฟฟ้า

apply, to (for permission) khǎw
anúyâat ขออนุญาต

appointment nátmǎi นัดหมาย

approach, to (in space) khâo hǎa
เข้าหา

approach, to (in time) klâi wehlaa
ใกล้เวลา

appropriate màwsǒm เหมาะสม

approximately pramaan ประมาณ

April mehsǎayon เมษายน

architecture satǎapàtyákam
สถาปัตยกรรม

area phúehn thîi พื้นที่

argue, to thǐang เถียง

argument thaláw ทะเลาะ

arm khǎehn แขน

armchair kâw-îi tháo khǎehn
เก้าอี้เท้าแขน

army thahǎan bòk ทหารบก

around (approximately) raw raaw
ราวๆ

around (nearby) thǎeo níi แถวนี้

around (surrounding) râwp râwp
รอบๆ

arrange, to càtkaan จัดการ

arrangements, planning
kaan càtkaan, kaan waang phǎen
การจัดการ, การวางแผน

arrival kaan maa thǔeng การมาถึง

arrive, to maa thǔeng มาถึง

art sǐnlapà ศิลปะ

article (in newspaper)
bòt khwaam บทความ

artificial thiam เทียม
artist sĭnlábin ศิลปิน
ashamed, embarrassed
  nâa lá-ai น่าละอาย
Asia ehsia เอเชีย
ask about, to thăam kìaw kàp
  ถามเกี่ยวกับ
ask for, request khăw ขอ
asleep nawn làp นอนหลับ
assemble, gather rûap ruam
  รวบรวม
assemble, put together prakàwp
  ประกอบ
assist, to chûai ช่วย
assistance khwaam chûai lŭea
  ความช่วยเหลือ
astonished pralàat cai ประหลาดใจ
as well dûai ด้วย
at thîi ที่
at home thîi bâan ที่บ้าน
atmosphere, ambience
  banyaakàat บรรยากาศ
at night tawn klaang khuehn
  ตอนกลางคืน
at once than thii ทันที
attack (in war) cohm tii โจมตี
attack (with words) dàa wâa ด่าว่า
attain, reach thŭeng ถึง
attempt khwaam phayaayaam
  ความพยายาม
attempt, to phayaayaam พยายาม
attend, to khâo rûam เข้าร่วม
at the latest lâa sùt ล่าสุด
attitude thátsanákhatì ทัศนคติ
attractive nâa dueng dùut น่าดึงดูด
aubergine, eggplant makhŭea yao
  มะเขือยาว
auction, to pramuun ประมูล
auctioned off pramuun khăi
  ประมูลขาย
August sĭnghăakhom สิงหาคม
aunt (older) pâa ป้า
aunt (younger than mother) náa น้า
aunt (younger than father) aa อา

aunt (respectful address to an
  aging lady) khun pâa คุณป้า
Australia áwsàtrehlia ออสเตรเลีย
Australian khon áwsàtrehlia
  คนออสเตรเลีย
authority (person in charge)
  câw nâa thîi เจ้าหน้าที่
authority (power) amnâat อำนาจ
automobile, car rót yon รถยนต์
autumn rúeduu bai mái rûang
  ฤดูใบไม้ร่วง
available mii...hâi มี...ให้
available, to make càt hâi mii...
  จัดให้มี...
average (numbers) chalìa เฉลี่ย
average (so-so, just okay)
  ngán ngán งั้นๆ
awake tùehn khûen ตื่นขึ้น
awaken, wake someone up plùk
  ปลุก
aware rúu รู้
awareness khwaam ráp rúu
  ความรับรู้

B

baby thaarók ทารก
back (part of body) lăng หลัง
back up, to thăwi pai ถอยไป
back, rear lăng หลัง
back, to go klàp pai กลับไป
backward thăwi lăng ถอยหลัง
bad lehw เลว
bad luck suai ซวย
bag thŭng ถุง
baggage krapăo doehn thaang
  กระเป๋าเดินทาง
bake, to òp อบ
baked òp อบ
bald hŭa láan หัวล้าน
ball bawn บอล
ballpoint pàakkaa mùek hâeng
  ปากกาหมึกแห้ง
banana klûai กล้วย

bandage

bandage phalaasatôeh pìt phlǎeh พลาสเตอร์ปิดแผล

bangs, fringes rahai, khrui ระบาย, ครุย

bank (finance) thanaakhaan ธนาคาร

bank (of river) rim fàng mâeh náam ริมฝั่งแม่น้ำ

banquet ngaan líang งานเลี้ยง

bar (blocking way) khwǎang thaang ขวางทาง

bar (serving drinks) baa บาร์

barber châang tàt phǒm ช่างตัดผม

barely thâep ca mâi... แทบจะไม่...

bargain, to tàw rawng ต่อรอง

barren mâi mii prayòht ไม่มีประโยชน์

base, foundation thǎan ฐาน

based on yúet taam ยึดตาม

basic bûeang tôn เบื้องต้น

basis thǎan ฐาน

basket tàkrâa ตะกร้า

basketball baasakèhtbawn บาสเก็ตบอล

bath àang àap náam อ่างอาบน้ำ

bathe, take a bath àap náam อาบน้ำ

bathe, swim wâi náam ว่ายน้ำ

bathrobe sûea khlum àap náam เสื้อคลุมอาบน้ำ

bathroom hâwng náam ห้องน้ำ

battle sûu róp สู้รบ

bay àao อ่าว

be, exist yùu อยู่

beach chai hàat ชายหาด

bean thùa ถั่ว

beancurd tâo hûu เต้าหู้

beard khrao เครา

beat (to defeat) chaná, tham hâi pháeh ชนะ, ทำให้แพ้

beat (to strike) tii ตี

beautiful sǔai สวย

because phráw เพราะ

become, to klai pen กลายเป็น

bed tiang เตียง

bedding, bedclothes khrûeang nawn เครื่องนอน

bedroom hâwng nawn ห้องนอน

bedsheet phâa puu thîi nawn ผ้าปูที่นอน

beef núea เนื้อ

beer bia เบียร์

before (in front of) khâng nâa ข้างหน้า

before (in time) kàwn ก่อน

beforehand, earlier kàwn lûang nâa ก่อนล่วงหน้า

begin, to rôehm เริ่ม

beginning tawn rôehm tôn ตอนเริ่มต้น

behave pràphrúet ประพฤติ

behind khâng lǎng ข้างหลัง

belief, faith khwaam chûea ความเชื่อ

believe, to chûea เชื่อ

belongings sǎmphaará สัมภาระ

belong to pen khǎwng เป็นของ

below, downstairs khâng lâang ข้างล่าง

belt khěm khàt เข็มขัด

beside khâng khâang ข้าง ๆ

besides nâwk càak นอกจาก

best dii thîi sùt ดีที่สุด

best wishes dûai khwaam praathanǎa dii ด้วยความปรารถนาดี

better dii kwàa ดีกว่า

better, get (improve) dii khûen ดีขึ้น

better, get (be cured) khâwi yang chûa ค่อยยังชั่ว

between ráwàang ระหว่าง

bicycle rót cakrayaan รถจักรยาน

big yài ใหญ่

bill bin บิล

billion phan láan พันล้าน

bird nók นก

birth, to give khlâwt lûuk คลอดลูก

birthday wan kòeht วันเกิด

biscuit (salty, cracker) bitsakît บิสกิต

biscuit (sweet, cookie) khúkkîi คุ๊กกี้

bit (part) chín ชิ้น

bit (slightly) nít nàwi นิดหน่อย

bite, to kàt กัด

bitter khŏm ขม

black dam ดำ

black beans thùa dam ถั่วดำ

blame, to thôht โทษ

bland cùeht จืด

blanket phâa hòm ผ้าห่ม

blind taa bàwt ตาบอด

blood lûeat เลือด

blouse sûea เสื้อ

blue sĭi fáa สีฟ้า

board kradaan กระดาน

board, to (bus, train) khûen ขึ้น

boat ruea เรือ

body râang kai ร่างกาย

boil, to tôm ต้ม

boiling dùeat เดือด

bon voyage! doehn thaang doi plàwt phai ná เดินทางโดยปลอดภัยนะ

bone kradùuk กระดูก

book nangsŭeh หนังสือ

border, edge khàwp ขอบ

border (between countries) chai daen ชายแดน

bored bùea เบื่อ

boring nâa bùea น่าเบื่อ

born, to be kòeht เกิด

borrow, to khăw yuehm ขอยืม

boss nai นาย

botanic gardens bawtaaník kaaden บอตานิค การ์เด้นส์

both tháng khûu ทั้งคู่

both...and tháng...láe... ทั้ง... และ...

bother, disturb rópkuan รบกวน

bother, disturbance kaan rópkuan การรบกวน

bottle khùat ขวด

bottom (base) khâng tâi ข้างใต้

bottom (buttocks) kôn กัน

boundary, border chai daehn ชายแดน

bowl chaam ชาม

box klàwng กล่อง

box (cardboard) klàwng kradàat กล่องกระดาษ

boy dèk chai เด็กชาย

boyfriend phûean chai เพื่อนชาย

bra yok song ยกทรง

bracelet kamlai mueh สร้อย

brain sa-măwng สมอง

brake brèhk เบรค

brake, to yìap brèhk เหยียบเบรค

branch săakhăa สาขา

brave, daring klâa hăn กล้าหาญ

bread khanŏm pang ขนมปัง

break, shatter tàehk la-ìat แตกละเอียด

break apart, to tàehk yâehk แตกแยก

break down, to (car, machine) sĭa เสีย

breakfast, morning meal aahăan cháo อาหารเช้า

breakfast, to eat kin aahăan cháo กินอาหารเช้า

breast(s) nâa òk หน้าอก

bride câw săaw เจ้าสาว

bridegroom câw bàaw เจ้าบ่าว

bridge saphaan สะพาน

brief sân sân สั้น ๆ

briefcase krapăw tham ngaan กระเป๋าทำงาน

briefs sûea klâam เสื้อกล้าม

bright sawàang สว่าง

bring up (children) líang เลี้ยง

bring up (topic) sanŏeh เสนอ

bring, to aw maa เอามา

British angkrìt อังกฤษ

broad, spacious kwâang กว้าง

broadcast, program raikaan kracai sĭang รายการกระจายเสียง

broadcast, to kracai sĭang กระจายเสียง

B

broccoli bráwkkhawฦi บ็อคโคลี่

broken off (relationship)
lôehk kan เลิกกัน

broken, does not work, spoiled
sĭa เสีย

broken, shattered tàehk แตก

broken, snapped (of bones, etc.)
hàk หัก

bronze ngoen ทองสัมฤทธิ์

broom mái kwàat ไม้กวาด

broth, soup náam súp น้ำซุป

brother (older) phîi chai พี่ชาย

brother (younger) náwng chai
น้องชาย

brother-in-law (older) phîi khŏei
พี่เขย

brother-in-law (younger) náwng
khŏei น้องเขย

brown námtaan น้ำตาล

bruise chám ช้ำ

brush praehng แปรง

brush, to praehng แปรง

bucket krapăwng กระป๋อง

Buddhism sàatsanăa phút
ศาสนาพุทธ

Buddhist chao phút ชาวพุทธ

buffalo (water buffalo) khwai ควาย

build, to sâang สร้าง

building kaan kàw sâang
การก่อสร้าง

Burma phamâa พม่า

Burmese chao phamâa ชาวพม่า

burn (injury) phlăeh mâi แผลไหม้

burn, to phăo เผา

burned down, out mâi mòt
ไหม้หมด

bus rót meh รถเมล์

bus station sathăanii rót meh
สถานีรถเมล์

business thurákìt ธุรกิจ

businessperson nák thurákìt
นักธุรกิจ

busy (doing something) yûng ยุ่ง

busy (crowded) wûn wai วุ่นวาย

busy (telephone) săi mâi wâang
สายไม่ว่าง

but tàeh แต่

butter noei เนย

butterfly phĭi sŭea ผีเสื้อ

buttocks kôn ก้น

buy, to súeh ซื้อ

by (author, artist) doi โดย

by means of dûai wíthii ด้วยวิธี ...

by the way nâwk càak níi,
ìik yàang nueng นอกจากนี้,
อีกอย่างหนึ่ง

C

cabbage kalàm plii กะหล่ำปลี

cabbage, Chinese phàk kàat khăo
ผักกาดขาว

cake, pastry khanŏm khéhk
ขนมเค้ก

calculate khamnuan คำนวณ

calculator khrûeang khít lêhk
เครื่องคิดเลข

calf (lower leg) nâwng น่อง

call (s.o.) on the telephone mii
khon thoh maa มีคนโทร.มา

call, summon rîak เรียก

called, named chûeh ชื่อ

calm sangòp สงบ

Cambodia khamĕhn เขมร

Cambodian chao khamĕhn
ชาวเขมร

camera klâwng กล้อง

can, be able to săamâat สามารถ

can, may àat cà, àat ca อาจจะ

can, tin krapăwng กระป๋อง

cancel yók lôehk ยกเลิก

candle thian เทียน

candy, sweets tháwffii, tháwpfii
ท็อฟฟี่

capable of, to be săamâat
สามารถ

capture, to càp จับ

car, automobile rót รถ

cardboard kradàat khǎeng
กระดาษแข็ง

cards (game) phâi ไพ่

care for, love rák láe ao-cai sài
รักและเอาใจใส่

care of, to take duulaeh ดูแล

careful! rawang ระวัง

carpet phrom พรม

carrot khaehràwt แครอท

carry, to hîu หิ้ว

cart (horsecart) aan อาน

cart (pushcart) rót khěn รถเข็น

carve, to kàe salàk แกะสลัก

carving kaan kàe salàk การแกะสลัก

cash, money ngoen sòt เงินสด

cash a check, to lâehk chék
แลกเช็ค

cassette théhp kháasèt เทปคาสเซ็ท

cat maeo แมว

catch, to càp จับ

Catholic (Roman) lathí
khaathàwlík ลัทธิคาทอลิค

cauliflower dàwk kalàm ดอกกะหล่ำ

cause sǎahèht สาเหตุ

cautious rawag ระวัง

cave thâm ถ้ำ

CD sii dii ซีดี

CD-ROM sii dii rawm ซีดีรอม

ceiling phehdaan เพดาน

celebrate, to chalǎwng ฉลอง

celery khûenchài ขึ้นฉ่าย

cell phone mueh thǔeh มือถือ

center, middle trong klaang
ตรงกลาง

center (of city) klaang mueang
กลางเมือง

central sǔun klaang ศูนย์กลาง

century sattàwát ศตวรรษ

ceremony phíthii พิธี

certain, sure nâeh cai แน่ใจ

certainly! nâeh nawn แน่นอน

certificate prakàatsaniiyábàt
ประกาศนียบัตร

chair kâoîi เก้าอี้

challenge tháa thai ท้าทาย

champion chaehmpîan แชมเปี้ยน

chance, opportunity ohkàat
โอกาส

chance, by doi mâi tângcai
โดยไม่ตั้งใจ

change, small sèht sataang,
sèht stang เศษสตางค์

change, to (conditions, situations)
plìan เปลี่ยน

change, exchange (money)
lâehk plìan แลกเปลี่ยน

change, switch (clothes) plìan
เปลี่ยน

change one's mind plìan cai
เปลี่ยนใจ

character (personality)
bùkhalík láksanà บุคลิกลักษณะ

character (written) tua aksǎwn
ตัวอักษร

characteristic khunásombàt
คุณสมบัติ

chase, to lâi taam ไล่ตาม

chase away, chase out lâi pai
ไล่ไป

cheap thùuk ถูก

cheat, to kohng โกง

cheat, someone who cheats
khon kohng, khon khîi kohng
คนโกง, คนขี้โกง

check, verify trùat sàwp ตรวจสอบ

checked (pattern) lai màak rúk
ลายหมากรุก

cheek kâehm แก้ม

cheers! chai yoh ไชโย

cheese noei khǎeng เนยแข็ง

chess màak rúk หมากรุก

chest (box) hìip หีบ

chest (breast) nâa òk หน้าอก

chew, to khíao เคี้ยว

chicken kài ไก่

child (young person) dèk เด็ก

child (offspring) lûuk ลูก

chili pepper phrík พริก

C

chili sauce sáws phrík, sáwt phrík
ซอสพริก

chilled nǎo yen หนาวเย็น

chin khaang คาง

China mueang ciin เมืองจีน

Chinese khon ciin คนจีน

chocolate cháwkkohláet ช็อคโกแล็ต

choice thaang lûeak ทางเลือก

choose, to lûeak เลือก

chopsticks takìap ตะเกียบ

Christian khrístian, chao khrít
คริสเตียน, ชาวคริสต์

Christianity sàatsanǎa khrít
ศาสนาคริสต์

church bòht โบสถ์

cigar burìi siikaa บุหรี่ซิการ์

cigarette burìi บุหรี่

cilantro, coriander phàk chii ผักชี

cinema rohng nǎng โรงหนัง

circle wong klom วงกลม

citizen prachaachon ประชาชน

citrus (orange, lemon)
sôm, manao ส้ม, มะนาว

city mueang, krung เมือง, กรุง

class, category chán, praphêht
ชั้น, ประเภท

classes (at university) pii ปี

clean sa-àat สะอาด

clean, to tham khwaam sa-àat
ทำความสะอาด

cleanliness khwaam sa-àat
ความสะอาด

clear (of weather) plàwt pròhng
ปลอดโปร่ง

clever chalàat ฉลาด

climate banyaakàat บรรยากาศ

climb onto, into piin ปีน

climb up (hills, mountains)
tài, piin ไต่, ปีน

clock naalíkaa นาฬิกา

close together, tight tìt kan
ติดกัน

close to, nearby klâi ใกล้

close, to cover pìt ปิด

closed (door) pìt (pratuu) ปิด (ประตู)

closed (shop) pìt (ráan) ปิด (ร้าน)

closed (road) pìt (thanǒn) ปิด (ถนน)

cloth phâa ผ้า

clothes, clothing sûea phâa เสื้อผ้า

cloudy, overcast mûeht khrûem
มืดครึ้ม

cloves kaan phluu กานพลู

coat, jacket cáekkêt แจ็คเก็ต

coat, overcoat sûea nâwk เสื้อนอก

coconut máphráo มะพร้าว

coffee kaafae กาแฟ

coin rǐan, lǐan เหรียญ

cold yen เย็น

cold, flu wàt หวัด

cold weather nǎo หนาว

colleague, co-worker phûean
rûam ngaan เพื่อนร่วมงาน

collect payment, to ráp ngoen
duean รับเงินเดือน

college wíthayaalai วิทยาลัย

collide, to chon ชน

collision kaan chon การชน

color sǐi สี

comb wǐi หวี

come, to maa มา

come back klàp maa กลับมา

come in khâo maa เข้ามา

come on, let's go pai kan ไปกัน

comfortable sabaai สบาย

command, order kham sàng คำสั่ง

command, to sàng สั่ง

common, frequent thammadaa
ธรรมดา

company, firm bawrísàt บริษัท

compare, to prìap thîap เปรียบเทียบ

compared with prìap kàp เปรียบกับ

compete, to khàeng แข่ง

competition kaan khàeng khǎn
การแข่งขัน

complain, to bòn, ráwng thúk
บ่น, ร้องทุกข์

complaint kham ráwng thúk
คำร้องทุกข์

complete (finished) sămrèt สำเร็จ

complete (thorough)
doi sîn choehng โดยสิ้นเชิง

complete (whole) sŏmbuun,
khróp thûan สมบูรณ์, ครบถ้วน

complete, to tham hâi sèt ทำให้เสร็จ

completely yàang sŏmbuun
อย่างสมบูรณ์

complicated sáp sáwn ซับซ้อน

compose, write (letters, books,
music) tàeng, khĭan แต่ง, เขียน

composition, writings kaan tàeng,
kaan khĭan การแต่ง, การเขียน

compulsory phâak bangkháp
ภาคบังคับ

computer khawmphiutôeh
คอมพิวเตอร์

concentrate, to (liquid)
khêm khôn เข้มข้น

concentrate, to (think) mii
samaathí, tângcai มีสมาธิ, ตั้งใจ

concerning kìao kàp เกี่ยวกับ

condition (pre-condition)
ngûeankhăi เงื่อนไข

condition (status) saphâap สภาพ

confectionery khanŏm wăan
ขนมหวาน

confidence khwaam mâncai
ความมั่นใจ

confidence, to have mii khwaam
mâncai มีความมั่นใจ

Confucianism lathí khŏng cúeh
ลัทธิขงจื๊อ

confuse, to sàp sŏn สับสน

confused (in a mess) yûng
yŏehng ยุ่งเหยิง

confused (mentally) ngong, ngong
nguai งง, งงงวย

confusing nâa sàpsŏn น่าสับสน

congratulations! khăw sadaehng
khwaam yindii dûay ขอแสดงความ
ยินดีด้วย

connect together, to tìt tàw kan
ติดต่อกัน

conscious of, to be rúu sămnúek
รู้สำนึก

consider (to have an opinion)
phícaaránaa พิจารณา

consider (to think over) trài
trawng ไตร่ตรอง

consult, talk over with prùeksăa
ปรึกษา

contact, connection kaan tìt tàw
การติดต่อ

contact, get in touch with tìt tàw
ติดต่อ

continent tháwîip ทวีป

continue, to tham tàw pai ทำต่อไป

convenient sadùak สะดวก

conversation bòt sŏnthanaa
บทสนทนา

cook (person) khon tham aahăan
คนทำอาหาร

cook, to tham aahăan ทำอาหาร

cooked sùk สุก

cooker, stove tao เตา

cookie, sweet biscuit khúkkîi คุ้กกี้

cooking, cuisine kaan tham
aahăan การทำอาหาร

cool yen เย็น

cool, to tham hâi yen ทำให้เย็น

copper thawng daehng ทองแดง

copy sămnao สำเนา

coral hĭn pàkaarang หินปะการัง

coriander, cilantro phàk chii ผักชี

corn, grain khâo phôht ข้าวโพด

corner mum มุม

correct thùuk tâwng ถูกต้อง

correct, to kâeh hai thùuk แก้ให้ถูก

correspond (write letters)
khĭan còtmǎi เขียนจดหมาย

corridor thaang doehn nai tùek
ทางเดินในตึก

cost (expense) khâa chái cài
ค่าใช้จ่าย

cost (price) raakhaa ราคา

cotton fâi ฝ้าย

couch, sofa sohfâa โซฟา

C

cough kaan ai การไอ

cough, to ai ไอ

could, might àat cà, àat ca อาจจะ

count, reckon náp นับ

counter (for paying, buying tickets) kháwtôeh เคาน์เตอร์

country (nation) prathêht ประเทศ

country (rural area) chonabòt ชนบท

courgette, zucchini suukìnii ซูกินี

courtyard sanǎam yâa สนามหญ้า

cover, to pìt, khlum ปิด, คลุม

cow wua วัว

co-worker, colleague phûean rûam ngaan เพื่อนร่วมงาน

crab puu ปู

cracked tàehk แตก

cracker, salty biscuit khanǒmpang kràwp ขนมปังกรอบ

crafts ngaan fìimueh งานฝีมือ

craftsperson châang fìimueh ช่างฝีมือ

crate lang mái ลังไม้

crazy bâabâa bawbaw บ้าๆบอๆ

create, to sâang สร้าง

criminal àatyaakawn อาชญากร

cross, angry kròht, mohhǒh โกรธ, โมโห

cross, go over khâam ข้าม

crowded nâen แน่น

cruel dù rái ดุร้าย

cry, to ráwng hâi ร้องไห้

cry out, to takohn ตะโกน

cucumber taehng kwaa แตงกวา

cuisine, style of cooking kaan tham aahǎan การทำอาหาร

culture wattanátham วัฒนธรรม

cup thûai ถ้วย

cupboard tûu ตู้

cure (medical) yaa ráksǎa ยารักษา

cured, preserved (fruit) dawng ดอง

cured, preserved (foods) thanǎwm aahǎan ถนอมอาหาร

currency ngoen traa เงินตรา

curtains, drapes mâan ม่าน

custom, tradition thammaniam ธรรมเนียม

customer lûuk kháa ลูกค้า

cut, slice hàn หั่น

cut, to tàt ตัด

cute, appealing nâa rák น่ารัก

D

daily pracam wan ประจำวัน

damage chamrút, sǐa hǎi ชำรุด, เสียหาย

damage, to tham hǎi chamrút ทำให้ชำรุด

damp chúehn ชื้น

dance kaan tên ram การเต้นรำ

dance, to tên ram เต้นรำ

danger antarai อันตราย

dangerous nâa antarai น่าอันตราย

dark mûeht มืด

date (of the month) wan thîi วันที่

date of birth wan duean pii kòeht วันเดือนปีเกิด

daughter lûuk sǎo ลูกสาว

daughter-in-law lûuk saphái ลูกสะไภ้

dawn cháo trùu เช้าตรู่

day wan วัน

day after tomorrow maruehn níi มะรืนนี้

day before yesterday mûeawaan suehn níi เมื่อวานซืนนี้

daydream, to fǎn klaang wan ฝันกลางวัน

day off wan yùt วันหยุด

day of the week wan วัน

dead tai ตาย

deaf hǔu nùak หูหนวก

death khwaam tai ความตาย

debt nîi sǐn หนี้สิน

deceive, to làwk luang หลอกลวง

December thanwaakhom ธันวาคม

decide, to tàtsǐn cai ตัดสินใจ

decision kaan tàtsǐn cai การตัดสินใจ

D

decline (get less) lót long ลดลง

decline (refuse) patìsèht ปฏิเสธ

decorate, to tòp tàeng ตบแต่ง

decrease, to lót long ลดลง

deep lúek ลึก

defeat, to tham hâi pháeh ทำให้แพ้

defecate, to thài ถ่าย

defecate, to (colloq.) ùe, khîi อี, ขี้

defect khâw bòk phrâwng
ข้อบกพร่อง

defend (in war) pâwng kan ป้องกัน

defend (with words) kâeh tàang
แก้ต่าง

definite nâe nawn แน่นอน

degree, level rádàp ระดับ

degrees (temperature) ongsǎa องศา

delay tham hâi lâa cháa ทำให้ล่าช้า

delayed lâa cháa ล่าช้า

delicious aràwi อร่อย

deliver, to sòng ส่ง

demand, to rîak ráwng เรียกร้อง

depart, to àwk càak ออกจาก

department phanàehk แผนก

department store hâang
sapphasìnkháa ห้างสรรพสินค้า

departure kaan càak pai,
kaan àwk การจากไป, การออก

depend on, to khûen yùu kàp
ขึ้นอยู่กับ

deposit (leave behind with
someone) ngoen mát cam
เงินมัดจำ

deposit (put money in the bank)
ngoen fàak เงินฝาก

descendant thaayâat ทายาท

describe, to banyai บรรยาย

desert (arid land) thaleh sai
ทะเลทราย

desert, to abandon thíng ทิ้ง

desire khwaam praathanǎa
ความปรารถนา

desire, to yàak, praathanǎa
อยาก, ปรารถนา

desk tó โต๊ะ

dessert khǎwng wǎan ของหวาน

destination cùt mǎi plai thaang
จุดหมายปลายทาง

destroy, to tham lai ทำลาย

destroyed, ruined thùuk tham lai
ถูกทำลาย

detergent phǒng sák fâwk
ผงซักฟอก

determined, stubborn dûeh ดื้อ

develop, to (happen) phátanaa
พัฒนา

develop, to (film) láang ล้าง

development kaan phátanaa
การพัฒนา

diagonal sên thá-yaehng mum
เส้นทแยงมุม

diagonally thá-yaehng mum ทแยงมุม

dial, to (telephone) mǔn หมุน

dialect phaasǎa thìn ภาษาถิ่น

diamond phét เพชร

diary, daybook samùt dai-aarîi
สมุดไดอารี่

diary, journal banthúek khào
pracam wan บันทึกข่าวประจำวัน

dictionary phótcanaanúkrom
พจนานุกรม

die, to tai ตาย

diet, to lót námnàk ลดน้ำหนัก

difference (discrepancy in figures)
phòn tàang ผลต่าง

difference (in quality) khwaam
tàek tàang ความแตกต่าง

different, other ùehn อื่น

difficult yâak ยาก

dinner, evening meal aahǎan yen
อาหารเย็น

dinner, to eat thaan aahǎan yen
ทานอาหารเย็น

dipper, ladle thápphii ทัพพี

direct, non-stop trong ตรง

direction thaang kham náenam
ทาง, คำแนะนำ

director (of company) phûu
amnuaikaan ผู้อำนวยการ

dirt, filth fùn ฝุ่น

dirty sòkkapròk สกปรก

disappointed phìt wăng ผิดหวัง

disaster phai phíbàt ภัยพิบัติ

discount lót raakhaa ลดราคา

discover, to khón phóp ค้นพบ

discuss, to thòk panhăa ถกปัญหา

discussion kaan thòk panhăa
การถกปัญหา

disease rôhk โรค

disgusting nâa rangkìat น่ารังเกียจ

dish, platter caan จาน

dish (particular food) caan จาน

diskette phàen dìs แผ่นดิสก์

dislike, to mâi châwp ไม่ชอบ

display kaan sadaehng การแสดง

display, to sadaehng แสดง

distance khwaam hàang klai
ความห่างไกล

disturb, to rópkuan รบกวน

disturbance khwaam mâi sangòp
ความไม่สงบ

divide, split up yâehk แยก

divided by hăan dûai หารด้วย

divorce, to yàa หย่า

divorced yàa láeo หย่าแล้ว

do, perform an action tham ทำ

don't! yàa อย่า

don't mention it mâi pen rai
ไม่เป็นไร

do one's best tham dii thîi sùt
ทำดีที่สุด

doctor măw หมอ

document, letter èhkasăan เอกสาร

dog măa หมา

done (cooked) sùk láeo สุกแล้ว

done (finished) sèt láeo เสร็จแล้ว

door pratuu ประตู

double săwng thâo สองเท่า

doubt, to sŏngsăi สงสัย

down, downward long maa ลงมา

downstairs khâng lâang ข้างล่าง

downtown nai mueang ในเมือง

dozen lŏh โหล

drapes, curtains mâan ม่าน

draw, to wâat วาด

drawer línchák ลิ้นชัก

drawing rûup wâat รูปวาด

dream khwaam făn ความฝัน

dream, to făn ฝัน

dress, frock chút sûea phâa
ชุดเสื้อผ้า

dressed, to get tàeng tua แต่งตัว

dressing gown sûea khlum
เสื้อคลุม

drink, refreshment khrûeang
dùehm เครื่องดื่ม

drink, to dùehm ดื่ม

drive, to (a car) khàp ขับ

driver khon khàp คนขับ

drought hâehng láehng แห้งแล้ง

drown, to tham hâi com náam
ทำให้จมน้ำ

drug (medicine) yaa ยา

drug (recreational) yaa bâa ยาบ้า

drugstore, pharmacy ráan khăi
yaa ร้านขายยา

drunk mao เมา

dry hâehng แห้ง

dry (weather) hâehng láehng
แห้งแล้ง

dry, to tham hâi hâehng ทำให้แห้ง

dry out (in the sun) tàak hâehng
ตากแห้ง

duck pèt เป็ด

dull (boring) nâa bùea น่าเบื่อ

dull (weather) khamùk khamŭa
ขมุกขมัว

dumpling (meat) pâehng yát sâi
núea แป้งยัดไส้เนื้อ

durian thurian ทุเรียน

during, between rawàang ระหว่าง

dusk châo mûeht ตอนโพล้เพล้

dust fùn ฝุ่น

duty (import tax) phaasĭi ภาษี

duty (responsibility) nâa thîi
หน้าที่

DVD dii wii dii ดีวีดี

E

each, every tàeh lá, thúk แต่ละ, ทุก

ear hǔu หู

earlier, beforehand kàwn níi ก่อนนี้

early reo kwàa pòkkatì เร็วกว่าปกติ

early in the morning cháo truu
  เช้าตรู่

earn, to hǎa maa dâi หามาได้

earrings tûm hǔu ตุ้มหู

earth, soil din ดิน

Earth, the world lôhk โลก

earthquake phàen din wǎi
  แผ่นดินไหว

east tawan àwk ตะวันออก

easy ngâi ง่าย

eat, to kin กิน

economical yàang prayàt
  อย่างประหยัด

economy sèhthakìt เศรษฐกิจ

edge khàwp ขอบ

educate, to sùeksǎa ศึกษา

education kaan sùeksǎa การศึกษา

effect, result phǒn ผล

effort khwaam phayaayaam
  ความพยายาม

effort, to make an phayaayaam
  พยายาม

egg khài ไข่

eggplant, aubergine makhǔea yao
  มะเขือยาว

eight pàeht แปด

eighteen sìp pàeht สิบแปด

eighty pàeht sìp แปดสิบ

either...or mâi... kâw... ไม่...ก็...

elbow khâw sàwk ข้อศอก

elder kàeh kwàa แก่กว่า

election kaan lûeak tâng การเลือกตั้ง

electric fai fáa ไฟฟ้า

electricity fay fáa ไฟฟ้า

electronic ilék thrawník อิเล็กทรอนิค

elegant yìng หยิ่ง

elephant cháang ช้าง

elevator líf ลิฟต์

eleven sìp èt สิบเอ็ด

else: anything else arai ìik
  อะไรอีก

else: or else rǔeh mâi kâw...
  หรือไม่ก็ ...

email (message) iimeh(l) อีเมล์

email (system) rabòp iimeh(l)
  ระบบอีเมล์

email address thîi yùu iimeh(l)
  ที่อยู่อีเมล์

email, to sòng iimeh(l) ส่งอีเมล์

embarrassed ai อาย

embarrassing nâa lá-ai น่าละอาย

embassy sathǎan thûut สถานทูต

embrace, to kàwt กอด

embroidered pàk ปัก

embroidery yép pàk thàk ráwi
  เย็บปักถักร้อย

emergency chùk chǒehn ฉุกเฉิน

emotion aarom อารมณ์

empty wâang plào ว่างเปล่า

end (tip) plaay ปลาย

end (finish) còp จบ

end, to sèt sîn เสร็จสิ้น

enemy sàtruu ศัตรู

energy phlang ngaan พลังงาน

engaged (telephone) sǎi mâi
  wâang สายไม่ว่าง

engaged (to be married) mân
  หมั้น

engine khrûeang yon เครื่องยนต์

England angkrìt อังกฤษ

English phaasǎa angkrìt ภาษาอังกฤษ

engrave, to salàk สลัก

enjoy, to sanùk สนุก

enjoyable nâa sanùk น่าสนุก

enjoy oneself, to tham tua hâi
  sanùk ทำตัวให้สนุก

enlarge, to khayǎi ขยาย

enough phaw พอ

enquire, to thǎam ถาม

enter, to khâo เข้า

entire tháng mòt ทั้งหมด

entirety, whole tháng mòt ทั้งหมด

E

entrance, way in thaang khâo ทางเข้า

envelope sawng ซอง

envious nâa ìtchǎa น่าอิจฉา

environment, the sìng wâeht láwm สิ่งแวดล้อม

envy khwaam rítsayǎa อิจฉา

equal thâo thiam เท่าเทียม

equality khwaam thâo thiam ความเท่าเทียม

error khwaam phìt ความผิด

escalator bandai lûan บันไดเลื่อน

especially doi chapháw โดยเฉพาะ

essay riang khwaam เรียงความ

establish, set up kàw tâng ก่อตั้ง

estimate, to pramaan ประมาณ

ethnic group chon klùm náwi ชนกลุ่มน้อย

Europe yúròhp ยุโรป

even (also) máeh tàeh แม้แต่

even (smooth) rîap เรียบ

evening tawn yen ตอนเย็น

event hèht kaan เหตุการณ์

ever, have already khoei เคย

every thúk ทุก

everybody, everyone thúk khon ทุกคน

every kind of thúk chanít ทุกชนิด

everything thúk sìng ทุกสิ่ง

every time thúk thii ทุกที

everywhere thúk thîi ทุกที่

exact, exactly nâeh nawn แน่นอน

exactly! just so! nân làe นั่นแหละ

exam, test kaan sàwp การสอบ

examine, to sàwp สอบ

example tua yàang ตัวอย่าง

example, for chên เช่น

excellent yâwt yîam ยอดเยี่ยม

except nâwk càak นอกจาก

exchange, to (money, opinions) lâek plìan แลกเปลี่ยน

exchange rate atraa lâehk plìan อัตราแลกเปลี่ยน

excited tùehn tên ตื่นเต้น

exciting nâa tùehn tên น่าตื่นเต้น

excuse me! (attracting attention) khǎw thôht ขอโทษ

excuse me! (getting past) khǎw thaang nàwi ขอทางหน่อย

excuse me! (apology) khǎw thôht ขอโทษ

exist, to yùu อยู่

exit, way out thaang àwk ทางออก

expand, grow larger khayǎi ขยาย

expect, to khâat wâa... คาดว่า...

expense rai cài รายจ่าย

expenses khâa chái cài ค่าใช้จ่าย

expensive phaehng แพง

experience prasòpkaan ประสบการณ์

experience, to mii prasòp kaan มีประสบการณ์

expert chamnaan ชำนาญ

explain, to athíbai อธิบาย

export kaan sòng àwk การส่งออก

export, to sòng àwk ส่งออก

express, urgent dùan ด่วน

express, state sadaehng แสดง

extension (telephone) tàw ต่อ

extra phôehm เพิ่ม

extremely sùt khùa สุดขั้ว

eye taa ตา

eyebrow khíu คิ้ว

eyeglasses, spectacles wâen sǎi taa แว่นสายตา

F

fabric, textile phâa ผ้า

face nâa หน้า

face, to phachoehn nâa เผชิญหน้า

fact khâw thét cing ข้อเท็จจริง

factory rohng ngaan โรงงาน

fail, to mâi prasòp phòn sǎmrèt ไม่ประสบผลสำเร็จ

failure khwaam lóm lěo ความล้มเหลว

fall (season) rúeduu bai mái rûang ฤดูใบไม้ร่วง

fall, to tòk ตก
fall over hòk lóm หกล้ม
false (imitation) thiam เทียม
false (not true) phìt ผิด
family khrâwp khrua ครอบครัว
famine khwaam òt yàak
  ความอดหยาก
famous dang ดัง
fan (admirer) faehn แฟน
fan (for cooling) phátlom พัดลม
fancy faensîi แฟนซี
far klai ไกล
fare khâa doisǎan ค่าโดยสาร
fast, rapid reo เร็ว
fast, to òt aahǎan อดอาหาร
fat, grease khǎi man ไขมัน
fat, plump ûan อ้วน
father phâw พ่อ
father-in-law phâw taa พ่อตา
fault khwaam phìt ความผิด
fax (machine) fáek(s) แฟ็กซ์
fax (message) fáek(s) แฟ็กซ์
fax, to sòng fáek(s) ส่งแฟ็กซ์
fear khwaam klua ความกลัว
February kumphaaphan กุมภาพันธ์
fee khâa thammaniam ค่าธรรมเนียม
feed, to hâi aahǎan ให้อาหาร
feel, to rúusùek รู้สึก
feeling khwaam rúusùek ความรู้สึก
feeling cold nǎw หนาว
female yǐng หญิง
fence rúa รั้ว
ferry ruea khâam fâak เรือข้ามฟาก
fertile udom อุดม
festival thêhtsakaan เทศกาล
fetch, to pai ao maa ไปเอามา
fever khâi ไข้
few mâi kìi... ไม่กี่...
few, a sǎwng sǎam สองสาม
fiancé, fiancée khûu mân คู่มั่น
field, empty space sanǎam สนาม
fierce dù ดุ
fifteen sìp hâa สิบห้า
fifty hâa sìp ห้าสิบ

fight, to (physically) sûu สู้
fight over, to yâehng แย่ง
figure, number tua lêhk ตัวเลข
fill, to toehm เติม
fill out (form) kràwk กรอก
film (camera) fiim ฟิล์ม
film, movie nǎng หนัง
final sùt thái สุดท้าย
finally nai thîisùt ในที่สุด
find, to phóp พบ
fine (okay) dii ดี
fine (punishment) khâa pràp ค่าปรับ
finger níu นิ้ว
finish sèt เสร็จ
finish off, to tham hâi sèt ทำให้เสร็จ
finished (complete) sèt láeo
  เสร็จแล้ว
finished (none left) mòt láeo
  หมดแล้ว
fire fai ไฟ
fire someone, to lâi àwk ไล่ออก
fireworks prathát ประทัด
firm, company bawrísàt บริษัท
firm (mattress) khǎeng แข็ง
firm (definite) mânkhong มั่นคง
first râehk แรก
first, earlier, beforehand kàwn ก่อน
fish plaa ปลา
fish, to tòk plaa ตกปลา
fish paste kapì กะปิ
fish sauce nám plaa น้ำปลา
fit, to sày phaw dii ใส่พอดี
fitting, suitable màw sòm เหมาะสม
five hâa ห้า
fix, to (a time, appointment) nát
  นัด
fix, to (repair) kâeh แก้
flag thong ธง
flashlight, torch fai chǎi ไฟฉาย
flat, apartment flàet แฟลต
flat, smooth rîap เรียบ
flight thîao bin เที่ยวบิน
flood náam thûam น้ำท่วม
floor phúehn พื้น

flour

flour pâehng แป้ง

flower dàwk mái ดอกไม้

flu khâi wàt yài ไข้หวัดใหญ่

fluent khlâwng คล่อง

flute khlùi ขลุ่ย

fly (insect) malaehngwan แมลงวัน

fly, to bin บิน

fog màwk หมอก

fold, to pháp พับ

follow along, to taam ตาม

follow behind, to taam lǎng
ตามหลัง

following dang tàw pai níi ดังต่อไปนี้

fond of, to be châwp ชอบ

food aahǎan อาหาร

foot tháo เท้า

for sǎmràp สำหรับ

forbid, to hâam ห้าม

forbidden tâwng hâam ต้องห้าม

force kamlang กำลัง

force, compel bangkháp บังคับ

forehead nâa phàak หน้าผาก

foreign tàang prathêht ต่างประเทศ

foreigner chao tàang prathêht
ชาวต่างประเทศ

forest pàa ป่า

for ever talàwt pai ตลอดไป

forget about, to luehm kìao kàp
ลืมเกี่ยวกับ

forget, to luehm ลืม

forgive, to hâi aphai ให้อภัย

forgiveness, mercy kaan hâi aphai
การให้อภัย

forgotten thùuk luehm ถูกลืม

fork sâwm ซ่อม

form (shape) rûup râang รูปร่าง

form (to fill out) kràwk bàehp
fawm กรอกแบบฟอร์ม

fortress pâwm, praasàat ป้อม,
ปราสาท

fortress wall kamphaehng praasàat
กำแพงปราสาท

fortunately chôhk dii thîi...
โชคดีที่...

forty sìi sìp สี่สิบ

forward pai khâng nâa ไปข้างหน้า

four sìi สี่

fourteen sìp sìi สิบสี่

free of charge mâi khít ngoen
ไม่คิดเงิน

free of commitments mâ mii
khâw phùuk mát ไม่มีข้อผูกมัด

free, independent ìtsarà อิสระ

freedom ìtsaràphâap อิสรภาพ

freeze châeh khǎeng แช่แข็ง

frequent bàwi บ่อย

fresh sòt สด

Friday wan sùk วันศุกร์

fried thâwt ทอด

friend phûean เพื่อน

friendly, outgoing pen kan ehng
เป็นกันเอง

frightened tòk cai ตกใจ

from càak จาก

front khâng nâa ข้างหน้า

front: in front of khâng nâa ข้างหน้า

frown kaan khamùat khíu
การขมวดคิ้ว

frown, to khamùat khíu ขมวดคิ้ว

frozen châeh khǎeng แช่แข็ง

fruit phǒnlamái ผลไม้

fry, to thâwt ทอด

fulfill sǎmrèt สำเร็จ

full tem เต็ม

full, eaten one's fill ìm อิ่ม

fun, to have sanùk สนุก

function, to work tham ngaan
ทำงาน

funds, funding thun ทุน

funeral ngaan sòp งานศพ

fungus chúea raa เชื้อรา

funny talòk ตลก

furniture foehnítcoeh เฟอร์นิเจอร์

further, additional phôehm toehm
เพิ่มเติม

fussy rûeang mâak เรื่องมาก

future: in future nai anaakhót
ในอนาคต

G

gamble kaan phanan การพนัน
game kehm เกม
garage (for repairs) ùu sôm rót
อู่ซ่อมรถ
garage (for parking) rohng rót
โรงรถ
garbage kha-yà ขยะ
garden, yard sǔan สวน
gardens, park sǔan sǎathaaraná
สวนสาธารณะ
garlic krathiam กระเทียม
garment sûea phâa เสื้อผ้า
gasoline námman น้ำมัน
gasoline station pám námman
ปั๊มน้ำมัน
gate pratuu ประตู
gather, to rûap ruam รวบรวม
gender phêht เพศ
general, all-purpose thûa pai ทั่วไป
generally doi thûa pai โดยทั่วไป
generous cai kwâang ใจกว้าง
gentle àwn yohn อ่อนโยน
gesture thâa thaang ท่าทาง
get off (transport) long ลง
get on (transport) khûen ขึ้น
get up (from bed) lúk khûen
ลุกขึ้น
get well soon! hǎi wai wai
หายไว ๆ
get, receive dâi ráp ได้รับ
ghost phǐi ผี
gift khǎwng khwǎn ของขวัญ
ginger khǐng ขิง
girl dèk phûu yǐng เด็กผู้หญิง
girlfriend faehn แฟน
give, to hâi ให้
given name chûeh ชื่อ
glad dii cai ดีใจ
glass (for drinking) kâeo แก้ว
glass (material) kracòk กระจก
glasses, spectacles wâen taa
แว่นตา

glutinous rice khâo nǐao
ข้าวเหนียว
go, to pai ไป
go along, join in pai dûai ไปด้วย
go around, visit pai yîam ไปเยี่ยม
go back klàp pai กลับไป
go for a walk pai doehn lên
ไปเดินเล่น
go home klàp bâan กลับบ้าน
go out, exit àwk pai ออกไป
go out (fire, candle) dàp ดับ
go to bed pai nawn ไปนอน
go up, climb tài ไต่
goal pâo mǎi เป้าหมาย
goat pháe แพะ
God phrá phûu pen câo
พระผู้เป็นเจ้า
god phrá câo พระเจ้า
goddess câo mâeh เจ้าแม่
gold thawng ทอง
golf káwf กอล์ฟ
gone, finished mòt láeo หมดแล้ว
good dii ดี
goodbye laa kàwn ลาก่อน
good luck! chôhk dii โชคดี
goodness! ôh hoh โอ้โฮ
goose hàan ห่าน
government ráttabaan รัฐบาล
gradually thii la nít ทีละนิด
grand, great yîng yài ยิ่งใหญ่
grandchild lǎan หลาน
granddaughter lǎan sǎo หลานสาว
grandfather (paternal) pùu ปู่
grandfather (maternal) taa ตา
grandmother (paternal) yâa ย่า
grandmother (maternal) yai ยาย
grandparents pùu yâa taa yai
ปู่ย่าตายาย
grandson lǎan chai หลานชาย
grapes angùn อุ่น
grass yâa หญ้า
grateful sâap súeng ซาบซึ้ง
grave lǔm sòp หลุมศพ
gray sǐi thao สีเทา

G

great, impressive pratháp cai
ประทับใจ

Greater vehicle of Buddhism,
Mahayana lathí mahǎayaan
ลัทธิมหายาน

green khǐao เขียว

green beans thùa fàk yao ถั่วฝักยาว

greens phàk sǐi khǐao ผักสีเขียว

greet, to thák thai ทักทาย

greetings kaan thák thai
การทักทาย

grill, to pîng ปิ้ง

ground, earth din ดิน

group klùm กลุ่ม

grow, be growing (plant) toh โต

grow, cultivate plùuk ปลูก

grow larger, to toh khûen โตขึ้น

grow up (child) toh โต

guarantee prakan ประกัน

guarantee, to prakan ประกัน

guard, to fâo yaam เฝ้ายาม

guess, to dao เดา

guest khàehk แขก

guesthouse ruean ráprawng khàek
เรือนรับรองแขก

guest of honour khàek phûu mii
kìat แขกผู้มีเกียรติ

guide, lead nam นำ

guidebook nangsǔeh nam thîao
หนังสือนำเที่ยว

guilty (of a crime) phìt ผิด

guilty, to feel rúusùek phìt รู้สึกผิด

H

hair phǒm ผม

half khrûeng ครึ่ง

hall hâwng thǒhng ห้องโถง

hand mueh มือ

handicap phíkaan พิการ

handicraft kaan fìimueh การฝีมือ

handle thîi thǔeh ที่ถือ

hand out càek แจก

hand over mâwp hâi มอบให้

handsome làw หล่อ

hang, to khwǎehn แขวน

happen, occur kòeht khûen เกิดขึ้น

happened, what happened?
kòeht arai khûen เกิดอะไรขึ้น

happening, incident hèht kaan
เหตุการณ์

happy mii khwaam sùk มีความสุข

happy birthday! sùksǎn wan kòeht
สุขสันต์วันเกิด

happy new year! sùksǎn wan pii
mày สุขสันต์วันปีใหม่

harbor thâa ruea ท่าเรือ

hard (difficult) yâak ยาก

hard (solid) khǎeng แข็ง

hard disk haaddís ฮาร์ดดิสก์

hardly thâehp ca mâi แทบจะไม่

hardworking, industrious khayàn
ขยัน

harmonious râap rûehn ราบรื่น

hat mùak หมวก

hate, to klìat เกลียด

hatred khwaam klìat ความเกลียด

have, own mii มี

have been somewhere khoei pai
เคยไป

have done something khoei tham
เคยทำ

have to, must tâwng ต้อง

he, him kháo เขา

head hǔa หัว

head for, toward mûng pai มุ่งไป

headdress khrûeang pradàp sìisà
เครื่องประดับศรีษะ

healthy sǒmbuun สมบูรณ์

hear, to dâi-yin ได้ยิน

heart hǔa cai หัวใจ

heat, to tham hâi ráwn ทำให้ร้อน

heavy nàk หนัก

height khwaam sǔung ความสูง

hello, hi sawàt dii สวัสดี

hello! (on phone) hal-lòh ฮัลโหล

help! chûai dûai ช่วยด้วย

help, to chûai ช่วย

her kháo เขา

hers khǎwng kháo ของเขา

here thîi nîi ที่นี่

hidden sâwn yùu ซ่อนอยู่

hide, to àehp แอบ

high sǔung สูง

hill noehn khǎo เนินเขา

hinder, to kìit khwǎang กีดขวาง

hindrance sìng kìit khwǎang
สิ่งกีดขวาง

hire, to châo เช่า

his khǎwng kháo ของเขา

history prawàt-sàat ประวัติศาสตร์

hit, strike tii ตี

hobby ngaan adirèhk งานอดิเรก

hold, to grasp yúet thǔeh ยึดถือ

hold back yùt wái หยุดไว้

hole ruu รู

holiday (festival) wan yùt
thêhtsakaan วันหยุดเทศกาล

holiday (vacation) wan yùt phák
phàwn วันหยุดพักผ่อน

holiday (public) wan yùt
râatchakaan วันหยุดราชการ

holy sàksìt ศักดิ์สิทธิ์

home, house bâan บ้าน

honest sûehsàt ซื่อสัตย์

honey nám phûeng น้ำผึ้ง

Hong Kong hâwng kong ฮ่องกง

hope, to wǎng หวัง

hopefully dûai khwaam wǎng
ด้วยความหวัง

horse máa ม้า

hospital rohng phayaabaan
โรงพยาบาล

host câo phâap เจ้าภาพ

hot (spicy) phèt เผ็ด

hot (temperature) ráwn ร้อน

hotel rohngraehm โรงแรม

hot spring náam phú ráwn น้ำพุร้อน

hour chûamohng ชั่วโมง

house bâan บ้าน

how? yàangrai, yang-ngai อย่างไร,
ยังไง

how are you? sabaai dii lǒeh?
สบายดีหรือ

however yàangrai kâw taam
อย่างไรก็ตาม

how long? (time) naan thâwrai
นานเท่าไร

how long? (length) yao thâwrai
ยาวเท่าไร

how many...? kìi... กี่...

how much? thâwrai เท่าไร

how old? aayú thâwrai อายุเท่าไร

huge yài ใหญ่

human manút มนุษย์

humid chúehn ชื้น

humorous khòp khǎn ขบขัน

hundred ráwi ร้อย

hundred thousand sǎehn แสน

hungry hǐu หิว

hurry up! reo reo เร็วๆ

hurt (injured) cèp เจ็บ

hurt, to (cause pain) tham hâi cèp
ทำให้เจ็บ

husband sǎamii สามี

hut, shack krathâwm กระท่อม

I

I, me chán ฉัน

ice nám khǎeng น้ำแข็ง

ice cream aiskhriim, aitiim
ไอศครีม

idea khwaam khít ความคิด

identical mǔeankan เหมือนกัน

if thâa ถ้า

ignore, to moehn chǒei เมินเฉย

ignorant lá loei, mâi rúu rûeang
ละเลย, ไม่รู้เรื่อง

illegal phìt kòtmǎi ผิดกฎหมาย

ill, sick pùai ป่วย

illness khwaam cèp pùai
ความเจ็บป่วย

imagine, to wâat phâap วาดภาพ

immediately than thii ทันที

impolite mâi sùphâap ไม่สุภาพ

import

import kaan nam khâo การนำเข้า

import, to ñam khâo นำเข้า

importance khwaam sămkhan
ความสำคัญ

important sămkhan สำคัญ

impossible pen pai mâi dâi
เป็นไปไม่ได้

impression, to make an
sâang khwaam pratháp cai
สร้างความประทับใจ

impressive pratháp cai ประทับใจ

in, at (space) nai, thîi ใน, ที่

in (time, years) phaainai ภายใน

in addition phôehm toehm เพิ่มเติม

in order that, so that phûea thîi
เพื่อที่

incense thûup ธูป

incident hèht kaan เหตุการณ์

included, including ruam tháng
รวมทั้ง

increase kaan phôehm khûen
การเพิ่มขึ้น

increase, to phôehm เพิ่ม

indeed! cing cing จริงๆ

indigenous chao phúehn mueang
ชาวพื้นเมือง

Indonesia indohnisia อินโดนิเซีย

Indonesian chao indohnisia
ชาวอินโดนิเซีย

inexpensive mây phaehng ไม่แพง

influence itthíphon อิทธิพล

influence, to mii itthíphon
มีอิทธิพล

inform, to câehng แจ้ง

information khâwmuun ข้อมูล

information booth tûu hâi
khâwmuun ตู้ให้ข้อมูล

inhabitant phûu yùu aasăi
ผู้อยู่อาศัย

inject, to chìit ฉีด

injection kaan chìit การฉีด

injured dâi ráp bàat cèp
ได้รับบาดเจ็บ

injury kaan bàat cèp การบาดเจ็บ

ink mùek หมึก

insane bâa bâa baw bàw บ้าๆ บอๆ

insect malaehng แมลง

inside khâng nai ข้างใน

inside of khâng nai ข้างใน

inspect, to trùat ตรวจ

instead of thaen thîi แทนที่

instruct, tell to do something
hâi kham náenam ให้คำแนะนำ

insult kaan duu thùuk การดูถูก

insult someone, to duu thùuk ดูถูก

insurance prakan ประกัน

intend, to tângcai ตั้งใจ

intended for sămràp สำหรับ

intention khwaam tângcai
ความตั้งใจ

interest (money) dàwk bîa ดอกเบี้ย

interest (personal) khwaam sŏncai
ความสนใจ

interested in sŏncai สนใจ

interesting nâa sŏncai น่าสนใจ

international naanaachâat นานาชาติ

Internet intoehnét อินเตอร์เน็ต

interpreter lâam ล่าม

intersection sìiyâehk สี่แยก

into sùu, nai สู่, ใน

introduce oneself, to
náenam tua ehng แนะนำตัวเอง

introduce someone, to
náenam tua แนะนำตัว

invent, to pradìt ประดิษฐ์

invitation kham choehn คำเชิญ

invite, to (ask along) chuan ชวน

invite, to (formally) choehn เชิญ

invoice bai kèp ngoen ใบเก็บเงิน

involve, to kìaw khâwng เกี่ยวข้อง

involved thîi kìaw khâwng
ที่เกี่ยวข้อง

Ireland ailaehn ไอร์แลนด์

Irish chao airít ชาวไอริช

iron lèk เหล็ก

iron, to (clothing) ñit sûea รีดเสื้อ

Islam ìtsalaam, ìslaam อิสลาม

island kàw เกาะ

ENGLISH–THAI

item, individual thing sìng สิ่ง

ivory ngaa cháang งาช้าง

J

jacket cáekkêt แจ๊คเก็ต

jail khúk คุก

jam yaehm แยม

January mókkaraakhom มกราคม

Japan yîipùn ญี่ปุ่น

Japanese chao yîipùn ชาวญี่ปุ่น

jaw kraam กราม

jealous ìtchǎa อิจฉา

jealousy khwaam ìtchǎa ความอิจฉา

jewelry khrûeang phét phlawi
เครื่องเพชรพลอย

job ngaan งาน

join together, to khâo ruâm เข้าร่วม

join, go along pai dûai ไปด้วย

joke phûut lên พูดเล่น

journalist nák khào นักข่าว

journey kaan doehn thaang
การเดินทาง

jug, pitcher yùeak เหยือก

juice nám phǒnlamái น้ำผลไม้

July karákadaakhom กรกฎาคม

jump, to kradòht กระโดด

June míthùnaayon มิถุนายน

jungle pàa ป่า

just now dĭao níi ehng เดี๋ยวนี้เอง

just, only thâo nán เท่านั้น

just, fair yútìtham ยุติธรรม

K

keep, to kèp เก็บ

key (to room) kuncaeh กุญแจ

key (computer) pâehn แป้น

keyboard (of computer) khiibàwd
คีย์บอร์ด

kidney tai ไต

kidney beans thùa daehng ถั่วแดง

kill, murder khâa ฆ่า

kilogram kilohkram กิโลกรัม

kilometer kilohméht กิโลเมตร

kind, good (of persons) cai dii ใจดี

kind, type praphêht ประเภท

king phrá-mahǎa-kasàt
พระมหากษัตริย์

king, Thai nai lǔang ในหลวง

kiss cùup จูบ

kiss, to cùup จูบ

kitchen khrua ครัว

kiwi fruit kiiwii frút กีวีฟรุต

knee khào เข่า

knife mîit มีด

knock, to kháw เคาะ

know, to rúu รู้

know, be acquainted with rúucàk
รู้จัก

knowledge khwaam rúu ความรู้

Korea, North kaolǐi nǔea เกาหลีเหนือ

Korea, South kaolǐi tâi เกาหลีใต้

Korean (person) khon kaolǐi
คนเกาหลี

L

lacking khàat ขาด

ladder bandai บันได

ladle, dipper krabuai กระบวย

lady suphâap satrii สุภาพสตรี

lake thaleh sàap ทะเลสาบ

lamb, mutton núea kàe เนื้อแกะ

lamp takiang ตะเกียง

land phúehn din พื้นดิน

land, to (plane) long ลง

lane (of a highway) lehn เลน

lane (alley) sawi ซอย

language phaasǎa ภาษา

Laos lao ลาว

Laotian khon lao คนลาว

large yài ใหญ่

last sùt thái สุดท้าย

last night mûea khuehn níi
เมื่อคืนนี้

last week aathít thîi láeo
อาทิตย์ที่แล้ว

L

last year pii thîi láeo ปีที่แล้ว
late sǎi สาย
late at night dùek ดึก
later thii lǎng ทีหลัง
laugh at, to hǔaráw yáw หัวเราะเยาะ
laugh, to hǔaráw หัวเราะ
laws, legislation kòtmǎi กฎหมาย
lawyer thanai ทนาย
layer chán ชั้น
lay the table càt tó จัดโต๊ะ
lazy khîi kìat ขี้เกียจ
lead (to be a leader) nam นำ
lead (to guide someone
  somewhere) nam pai นำไป
leader phûu nam ผู้นำ
leaf bai mái ใบไม้
leak, to rûea รั่ว
learn, to rian เรียน
least (smallest amount)
  náwi thîi sùt น้อยที่สุด
least: at least yàang náwi อย่างน้อย
leather nǎng หนัง
leave, depart àwk càak ออกจาก
leave behind by accident luehm
  ลืม
leave behind on purpose
  thíng wáy ทิ้งไว้
leave behind for safekeeping fàak
  ฝาก
lecture banyaai บรรยาย
lecturer (at university) khon
  lékchôeh คนเล็คเชอร์
left, remaining thîi lǔea ที่เหลือ
left-hand side sái mueh ซ้ายมือ
leg khǎa ขา
legal taam kòtmǎi ตามกฎหมาย
legend tamnaan ตำนาน
lemon, citrus manao มะนาว
lemongrass takhrái ตะไคร้
lend, to hâi yuehm ให้ยืม
length khwaam yao ความยาว
less (smaller amount) náwi kwàa
  น้อยกว่า
less, minus lóp ลบ

lessen, reduce lót long ลดลง
Lesser vehicle of Buddhism,
  Hinayana lathí hǐnayaan
  ลัทธิหินยาน
lesson bòt rian บทเรียน
let, allow anuyâat อนุญาต
lets (suggestion) kanthòe กันเถอะ
let someone know, to bàwk บอก
letter còtmǎi จดหมาย
level (even, flat) rîap เรียบ
level (height) chán ชั้น
level (standard) radàp ระดับ
library hâwng samùt ห้องสมุด
license (for driving) bai khàp khìi
  ใบขับขี่
license, permit bai anuyâat
  ใบอนุญาต
lick, to lia เลีย
lid fǎa ฝา
lie, tell a falsehood kohhòk โกหก
lie down, to nawn นอน
life chiiwít ชีวิต
lifetime talàwt chiiwít ตลอดชีวิต
lift, elevator líf ลิฟท์
lift (ride in car) pai sòng ไปส่ง
lift, raise yók ยก
light (not heavy) baw เบา
light (bright) sawàang สว่าง
light (lamp) fai ไฟ
lighter fai cháek ไฟแช็ค
lightning fáa phàa ฟ้าผ่า
like, as mǔean เหมือน
like, be pleased by châwp ชอบ
likewise mǔeankan เหมือนกัน
lime, citrus manao มะนาว
line (mark) sên เส้น
line (queue) khiu คิว
line up, to khâo khiu เข้าคิว
lips rim fǐi pàak ริมฝีปาก
liquor, alcohol lâo เหล้า
list rai chûeh รายชื่อ
listening fang yùu ฟังอยู่
listen to fang ฟัง
literature wannákhadii วรรณคดี

marry, get married

little (not much) náwi น้อย
little (small) lék เล็ก
live (be alive) mii chiiwít มีชีวิต
live (stay in a place) yùu อยู่
liver tàp ตับ
load phaará ภาระ
load (up), to bancù บรรจุ
located, to be tâng yùu ตั้งอยู่
lock mâeh kuncaeh แม่กุญแจ
lock, to láwk ล็อค
locked láwk láeo ล็อคแล้ว
lodge, bungalow (guest house)
   bangkaloh บังกะโล
lonely ngǎo เหงา
long (length) yao ยาว
long (time) naan นาน
look! duu sí ดูซิ
look at, see duu ดู
look, seem, appear duu thâa
   thaang ดูท่าทาง
look after duulaeh ดูแล
look for hǎa หา
look like duu mǔean ดูเหมือน
look out! rawang ระวัง
look up (find in book) hǎa หา
loose (wobbly, not tight) lǔam
   หลวม
loose (having freedom)
   pen ìtsarà เป็นอิสระ
lose, be defeated pháeh แพ้
lose, mislay tham hǎi ทำหาย
lose money, to sǐa ngoen เสียเงิน
lost (missing) hǎi หาย
lost (can't find way) lǒng (thaang)
   หลง (ทาง)
lost property khǎwng hǎi ของหาย
lots of yóe yáe เยอะแยะ
lottery láwttoehrîi ล็อตเตอรี่
loud dang ดัง
love khwaam rák ความรัก
love, to rák รัก
lovely nâa rák น่ารัก
low tàm ต่ำ
luck chôhk โชค

lucky chôhk dii โชคดี
luggage krapǎo กระเป๋า
lunch, midday meal aahǎan
   klaang wan อาหารกลางวัน
lunch, to eat thaan khâo thîang
   ทานข้าวเที่ยง
lungs pàwt ปอด
luxurious rǔu rǎa หรูหรา
lychee líncìi ลิ้นจี่

M

machine khrûeang yon เครื่องยนต์
machinery khrûeang càk เครื่องจักร
madam (term of address)
   khun nai คุณนาย
magazine waarasǎan วารสาร
mah jong maa cawng มาจอง
mail, post mehl เมล์
mail, to sòng ส่ง
main, most important sǎmkhan
   สำคัญ
mainly thîi sǎmkhan ที่สำคัญ
major (important) yài ใหญ่
make, to tham ทำ
make up, invent pradìt ประดิษฐ์
Malaysia maalehsia มาเลเซีย
Malaysian chao maalehsia
   ชาวมาเลเซีย
male chai ชาย
man phûu chai ผู้ชาย
manage, succeed càt kaan จัดการ
manager phûu càtkaan ผู้จัดการ
mango mamûang มะม่วง
mangosteen mangkhút มังคุด
manufacture, to phalìt ผลิต
many, much mâak มาก
map phǎehn thîi แผนที่
March miinaakhom มีนาคม
market talàat ตลาด
married tàeng-ngaan láeo
   แต่งงานแล้ว
marry, get married tàeng-ngaan
   แต่งงาน

ENGLISH—THAI

M

mask nâa kàak หน้ากาก

Mass (go to) (pay ruam) phíthii nai bòht ไปร่วมพิธีในโบสถ์

massage, to nûat นวด

mat sùea เสื่อ

match, game kehm เกม

matches máikhìit ไม้ขีด

material, ingredient wátsadù วัสดุ

matter, issue rûeang เรื่อง

matter, it doesn't mâi pen rai ไม่เป็นไร

mattress thîi nawn ที่นอน

May phrúetsaphaakhom พฤษภาคม

may àat อาจ

maybe àat cà, àat ca อาจจะ

meal múeh มื้อ

mean (cruel) hèn kàeh tua เห็นแก่ตัว

mean, to (intend) mii cèhtanaa มีเจตนา

mean, to (word) măi khwaam หมายความ

meaning khwaam măi ความหมาย

meanwhile khanà thîi ขณะที่

measure, to wát วัด

measurement kaan wát การวัด

meat núea เนื้อ

meatball lûuk chín ลูกชิ้น

medical thaang kaan phâeht ทางการแพทย์

medicine yaa ยา

meet, to phóp พบ

meeting prachum ประชุม

melon taehng แตง

member samaachík สมาชิก

memories khwaam song cam ความทรงจำ

mend, to sâwm ซ่อม

menstruate, to mii pracam duean มีประจำเดือน

mention, to klào thŭeng กล่าวถึง

menu mehnuu เมนู

merely phiang เพียง

mess, in a rók รก

message khâw khwaam ข้อความ

metal lèk เหล็ก

method wíthii วิธี

midday thîang wan เที่ยงวัน

middle, center sŭun klaang ศูนย์กลาง

middle: be in the middle of doing klaang กลาง

midnight thîang khuehn เที่ยงคืน

mild (not spicy) mâi phèt ไม่เผ็ด

mild (not severe) mâi run raehng ไม่รุนแรง

milk nom นม

million láan ล้าน

mind, brain samăwng สมอง

mind, to be displeased rangkìat รังเกียจ

minibus rót meh lék รถเมล์เล็ก

minor (not important) mâi sămkhan ไม่สำคัญ

minus lóp ลบ

minute naathii นาที

mirror kracòk กระจก

misfortune khráw ráai เคราะห์ร้าย

miss, to (bus, flight) phlâat พลาด

miss, to (loved one) khít thŭeng คิดถึง

missing (absent) khàat pai ขาดไป

missing (lost person) hăi หาย

mist, fog màwk หมอก

mistake khwaam phìt ความผิด

mistaken phìt phlâat ผิดพลาด

misunderstanding khâwcai phìt เข้าใจผิด

mix, to phasŏm ผสม

mobile phone thohrasàp mueh thŭeh โทรศัพท์มือถือ

modern than samăi ทันสมัย

modest, simple thammadaa ธรรมดา

moment (instant) chûa khanà ชั่วขณะ

moment ago mûea kîi níi เมื่อกี้นี้

moment (in a moment, just a moment) dĭao เดี๋ยว

Monday wan can วันจันทร์

money ngoen เงิน

monitor (of computer) mawnítôeh มอนิเตอร์

monkey ling ลิง

month ducan เดือน

monument anúsăawarii อนุสาวรีย์

moon duang can ดวงจันทร์

more (comparative) kwàa กว่า

more of (things) mâak kwàa มากกว่า

more or less mâi mâak mâi náwi ไม่มากไม่น้อย

morning cháo เช้า

mosque surào สุเหร่า

mosquito yung ยุง

most (superlative) thîi sùt ที่สุด

most (the most of) mâak thîi sùt มากที่สุด

mostly sùan yài ส่วนใหญ่

moth tua chiipakhăo ตัวชีปะขาว

mother mâeh แม่

mother-in-law mâeh yai, mâeh săamii แม่ยาย, แม่สามี

motor, engine mawtôeh, khrûeang yon มอเตอร์, เครื่องยนต์

motorcycle mawtoehsai มอเตอร์ไซค์

motor vehicle yaan yon ยานยนต์

mountain phuu khăo ภูเขา

mouse (animal) nŭu หนู

mouse (computer) máw เมาส์

moustache nùat หนวด

mouth pàak ปาก

move, to khlûean thîi เคลื่อนที่

move from one place to another yái ย้าย

movement, motion khwaam khlûean wăi ความเคลื่อนไหว

movie năng หนัง

movie house rohng năng โรงหนัง

much, many mâak มาก

muscle klâam núea กล้ามเนื้อ

museum phíphítthaphan พิพิธภัณฑ์

mushroom hèt เห็ด

music dontrii ดนตรี

Muslim mútsalim, múslim มุสลิม

must tâwng ต้อง

my, mine khăwng chán ของฉัน

myth lúek láp ลึกลับ

N

nail (finger, toe) lép เล็บ

nail (spike) tapuu ตะปู

naked plueai เปลือย

name chûeh ชื่อ

narrow khâehp แคบ

nation, country châat ชาติ

national hàeng châat แห่งชาติ

nationality sănchâat สัญชาติ

natural pen thammachâat เป็นธรรมชาติ

nature thammachâat ธรรมชาติ

naughty son ซน

nearby klâi ใกล้

nearly kùeap เกือบ

neat, orderly ñap ráwi เรียบร้อย

necessary campen จำเป็น

neck khaw คอ

necklace sâwi khaw ร้อยคอ

necktie nékthai เน็คไท

need khwaam campen ความจำเป็น

need, to campen จำเป็น

needle khêm เข็ม

neighbour phûean bâan เพื่อนบ้าน

neither mâi tháng ไม่ทั้ง

neither...nor... tháng...láe...mâi... ทั้ง...และ...ไม่...

nephew lăan chai หลานชาย

nest rang รัง

net taakhài ตาข่าย

network khruea khài เครือข่าย

never mâi khoei ไม่เคย

never mind! mâi pen rai ไม่เป็นไร

nevertheless yàangrai kâw taam อย่างไรก็ตาม

new mài ใหม่

news khào ข่าว

newspaper nangsǔeh phim หนังสือพิมพ์

New Zealand niwsiilaehn นิวซีแลนด์

next (in line, sequence) tàw pai ต่อไป

next to thàt pai ถัดไป

next week sàpdaa nâa สัปดาห์หน้า

next year pii nâa ปีหน้า

nice dii ดี

niece lǎan sǎo หลานสาว

night klaang khuehn กลางคืน

nightclothes chút nawn ชุดนอน

nightdress chút nawn ชุดนอน

nightly thúk khuehn ทุกคืน

nine kâo เก้า

nineteen sìp kâo สิบเก้า

ninety kâo sìp เก้าสิบ

no, not (with nouns) mâi mii ไม่มี

no, not (with verbs and adjectives) mâi ไม่

nobody mâi mii khrai ไม่มีใคร

noise sǐang เสียง

noisy sǐang dang เสียงดัง

nonsense rái sǎará ไร้สาระ

noodles kúai tǐao ก๋วยเตี๋ยว

noon tawn thîiang ตอนเที่ยง

normal pòkkatì ปกติ

normally doi pòkkatì โดยปกติ

north nǔea เหนือ

north-east tawan àwk chǐang nǔea ตะวันออกเฉียงเหนือ

north-west tawan tòk chǐang nǔea ตะวันตกเฉียงเหนือ

nose camùuk จมูก

nostril ruu camùuk รูจมูก

not mâi ไม่

not only...but also mâi phiang... tàeh yang... ไม่เพียง...แต่ยัง...

not yet yang ยัง

note (currency) thonabàt ธนบัตร

note (written) khǐan nóht เขียนโน้ต

notebook samùt สมุด

note down, to còt nóht จดโน้ต

nothing mâi mii arai ไม่มีอะไร

notice câehng khwaam แจ้งความ

notice, to sǎngkèht สังเกต

novel nawaníyai นวนิยาย

November phrúetsacìkaayon พฤศจิกายน

now dǐao níi เดี๋ยวนี้

nowadays samǎi níi สมัยนี้

nowhere mâi mii thîi nǎi ไม่มีที่ไหน

nude plueai เปลือย

numb chaa ชา

number boeh, mǎi lêhk เบอร์, หมายเลข

nylon nailawn ไนลอน

O

o'clock naalíkaa, mohng นาฬิกา, โมง

obedient nâa chûea fang น่าเชื่อฟัง

obey, to chûea fang เชื่อฟัง

object, thing sìng khǎwng สิ่งของ

object, to protest khát kháan คัดค้าน

occasionally baang khráng baang khrao บางครั้งบางคราว

occupation aachîip อาชีพ

ocean mahǎa samùt มหาสมุทร

October tulaakhom ตุลาคม

odor, bad smell mii klìn มีกลิ่น

of course nâeh nawn แน่นอน

of, from càak จาก

off (gone bad) sǐa เสีย

off (turned off) pìt láeo ปิดแล้ว

off: to turn something off pìt ปิด

offend tham hâi mâi phaw cai ทำให้ไม่พอใจ

offer, suggest sanǒeh, náenam เสนอ, แนะนำ

offering khâw sanǒeh ข้อเสนอ

office thîi tham ngaan ที่ทำงาน

official, formal câo nâa thîi เจ้าหน้าที่

officials (government) khâa râatchakaan ข้าราชการ

often bàwi บ่อย

oil námman น้ำมัน

okay tòklong ตกลง

old (of persons) kàeh แก่

old (of things) kào เก่า

olden times, in samǎi kàwn สมัยก่อน

older brother or sister phîi พี่

on, at bon บน

on (of dates) wan thîi วันที่

on (turned on) pòeht เปิด

on: to turn something on pòeht เปิด

on board khûen, yùu bon... ขึ้น, อยู่บน...

on fire fai mâi ไฟไหม้

on foot (coming, going) doehn maa, doehn pai เดินมา, เดินไป

on the way kamlang doehn thaang กำลังเดินทาง

on the whole thâa duu tángmòt ถ้าดูทั้งหมด

on time trong wehlaa ตรงเวลา

once nùeng thii หนึ่งที

one nùeng หนึ่ง

one-way ticket tǔa thîao diao ตั๋วเที่ยวเดียว

one who, the one which khon thîi... คนที่...

onion hǎwm yài หอมใหญ่

only phiang tàeh, thâonán เพียงแต่, เท่านั้น

open pòeht เปิด

open, to pòeht เปิด

opinion khwaam hěn ความเห็น

opponent fài trong khâam ฝ่ายตรงข้าม

opportunity ohkàat โอกาส

oppose, to tàw tâan ต่อต้าน

opposed, in opposition kháan ค้าน

opposite (facing) yùu trong khâam อยู่ตรงข้าม

opposite (contrary) trong khâam ตรงข้าม

optional lûeak dâi เลือกได้

or rǔeh, lǒeh หรือ

orange, citrus sôm ส้ม

orange (color) sǐi sôm สีส้ม

order (command) kham sàng คำสั่ง

order (placed for food, goods) bai sàng ใบสั่ง

order, sequence taam lamdàp ตามลำดับ

order, to command sàng สั่ง

order something, to sàng สั่ง

orderly, organized pen rabìap เป็นระเบียบ

organize, arrange càt kaan จัดการ

origin cùt rôehm tôn จุดเริ่มต้น

original tua cing ตัวจริง

originate, come from maa càak มาจาก

ornament khrûeang pradàp เครื่องประดับ

other ùehn อื่น

ought to khuan ควร

our khǎwng rao ของเรา

out àwk ออก

outside khâng nâwk ข้างนอก

outside of khâng nâwk ข้างนอก

oval (shape) rûup khài รูปไข่

oven tao òp เตาอบ

over, finished sèt เสร็จ

over: to turn over klàp กลับ

overcast, cloudy mêhk mâak เมฆมาก

overcome, to khrâwp khrawng ครอบครอง

overseas tàang prathêht ต่างประเทศ

over there thîi nôhn ที่โน่น

overturned (boat) lôm ล่ม

overturned (vehicle) ngǎi tháwng หงายท้อง

owe, to pen nîi เป็นหนี้

own, on one's khon diao คนเดียว

own, personal khǎwng sùan tua ของส่วนตัว

own, to pen câo khǎwng เป็นเจ้าของ

oyster hǎwi naang rom หอยนางรม

P

pack, to (luggage) kèp khǎwng เก็บของ

package hàw khǎwng ห่อของ

page nâa หน้า

paid cài láeo จ่ายแล้ว

pain cèp เจ็บ

painful cèp mâak เจ็บมาก

paint sǐi สี

paint, to (a painting) rabai sǐi ระบายสี

paint, to (house, furniture) thaa sǐi ทาสี

painting phâap wâat ภาพวาด

pair of, a nùeng khûu หนึ่งคู่

pajamas chút nawn ชุดนอน

palace wang วัง

palace (royal) phrárâatchawang พระราชวัง

pan mâw หม้อ

panorama phâap kwâang ภาพกว้าง

panties kaangkehng nai กางเกงใน

pants kaangkehng กางเกง

papaya malákaw มะละกอ

paper kradàat กระดาษ

parcel phátsadù พัสดุ

parcel, to hàw ห่อ

pardon me? what did you say? arai náa อะไรนะ

parents phâw mâeh พ่อแม่

park sǔan sǎathaaraná สวนสาธารณะ

park, to (car) càwt rót จอดรถ

part (not whole) sùan ส่วน

part (of machine) alài อะไหล่

participate, to mii sùan rûam มีส่วนร่วม

particularly, especially doi chapháw โดยเฉพาะ

partly sùan nùeng ส่วนหนึ่ง

partner (in business) hûn sùan หุ้นส่วน

partner (spouse) khûu sǒmrót คู่สมรส

party (event) ngaan งาน

party (political) phák พรรค

pass, go past phàan ผ่าน

pass, to (exam) sàwp phàan สอบผ่าน

passenger phûu doi sǎan ผู้โดยสาร

passionfruit phol saowaroté ผลเสาวรส

passport nǎngsǔeh doehn thaang หนังสือเดินทาง

past: go past phàan ผ่าน

past, former adìit อดีต

pastime ngaan adirèhk งานอดิเรก

patient (calm) òt thon อดทน

patient (doctor's) khon khâi คนไข้

pattern, design bàehp แบบ

patterned mii lai มีลาย

pay attention tângcai ตั้งใจ

pay, to cài จ่าย

payment ngoen cài เงินจ่าย

peace sǎntiphâap สันติภาพ

peaceful sangòp สงบ

peak, summit yâwt ยอด

peanut thùa lísòng ถั่วลิสง

pearl khài múk ไข่มุก

peas thùa ถั่ว

pedestrian crossing thaang máa lai ทางม้าลาย

peel, to pàwk ปอก

pen pàakkaa ปากกา

pencil dinsǎw ดินสอ

penis khuai ควย

people khon คน

pepper, black phrík thai พริกไทย

pepper, chili phrík พริก

percent, percentage poehsen เปอร์เซ็นต์

performance kaan patìbàt ngaan การปฏิบัติงาน

perfume nám hǎwm น้ำหอม

perhaps, maybe àat cà, àat ca อาจจะ

perhaps, probably baang thii บางที

period (end of a sentence) còp จบ

period (menstrual) pracam duean
ประจำเดือน

period (of time) rayá wehlaa
ระยะเวลา

permanent thǎawawn ถาวร

permit, license bai anúyâat
ใบอนุญาต

permit, to allow anúyâat อนุญาต

person khon คน

personality bùkhalík láksanà
บุคลิกลักษณะ

perspire, to ngùea àwk เหงื่อออก

pet animal sàt líang สัตว์เลี้ยง

petrol námman น้ำมัน

petrol station pám námman
ปั๊มน้ำมัน

pharmacy, drugstore
ráan khǎi yaa ร้านขายยา

Philippines filíppin ฟิลิปปินส์

photocopy sǎmnao สำเนา

photocopy, to thài sǎmnao
ถ่ายสำเนา

photograph rûup thài รูปถ่าย

photograph, to thài rûup ถ่ายรูป

pick, choose lûeak เลือก

pick up, to (someone) ráp รับ

pick up, lift (something) kèp
khûen เก็บขึ้น

pickpocket nák lúang krapǎo
นักล้วงกระเป๋า

pickpocket, to lúang krapǎo
ล้วงกระเป๋า

picture (movie) nǎng หนัง

picture rûup phâap รูปภาพ

piece, portion, section tawn ตอน

piece, item chín ชิ้น

pierce, penetrate thaehng แทง

pig mǔu หมู

pillow mǎwn หมอน

pills yaa ยา

pineapple sapparót สับปะรด

pink sǐi chomphuu สีชมพู

pitcher, jug yùeak เหยือก

pity: what a pity! nâa sǒngsǎan
น่าสงสาร

place thîi ที่

place, put waang วาง

plain (not fancy) rîap เรียบ

plain (level ground) thîi râap ที่ราบ

plan phǎehn แผน

plan, to waang phǎehn วางแผน

plane khrûeang bin เครื่องบิน

plant tôn mái ต้นไม้

plant, to plùuk ปลูก

plastic pláasatìk, pláastìk พลาสติค

plate caan จาน

play, to lên เล่น

play around lên pai thûa เล่นไปทั่ว

plead, to âwn wawn อ้อนวอน

plead, to (in court) hâi kaan
ให้การ

pleasant nâa yindii น่ายินดี

please (go ahead) choehn เชิญ

please (request for help) chûai
ช่วย

please (request for something)
khǎw ขอ

pleased yindii, diicai ยินดี, ดีใจ

plug (bath) plák ปลั๊ก

plug (electric) plák fai ปลั๊กไฟ

plum lûuk phlam ลูกพลัม

plus bùak บวก

pocket krapǎo กระเป๋า

point (in time) cùt จุด

point, dot cùt จุด

point out chíi ชี้

poison yaa phít ยาพิษ

poisonous mii phít มีพิษ

police tamrùat ตำรวจ

police officer cao nâa thîi tamrùat
เจ้าหน้าที่ตำรวจ

polish, to khàt ngao ขัดเงา

politics kaan mueang การเมือง

polite sùphâap สุภาพ

poor con จน

popular pen thîi níyom เป็นที่นิยม

population pracaakawn ประชากร

P

pork núea mǔu เนื้อหมู

port thâa ruea ท่าเรือ

portion, serve thîi ที่

possess, to pen cao khǎwng เป็นเจ้าของ

possessions sǒmbàt สมบัติ

possible pen pai dâi เป็นไปได้

possibly àat cà, àat ca อาจจะ

post office praisanii ไปรษณีย์

post, column sǎo เสา

post, mail còtmǎi จดหมาย

postcard praisaniiyábàt ไปรษณียบัตร

postpone, to lûean เลื่อน

postponed, delayed lûean àwk pai เลื่อนออกไป

pot mâw หม้อ

potato man มัน

poultry kài ไก่

pour, to rin ริน

power amnâat อำนาจ

powerful mii amnâat มีอำนาจ

practice kaan fùek hàt การฝึกหัด

practice, to fùek hàt ฝึกหัด

praise kham yók yâwng คำยกย่อง

praise, to yók yâwng ยกย่อง

prawn kûng กุ้ง

pray, to sùat mon สวดมนต์

prayer bòt sùat mon บทสวดมนต์

prefer, to châwp mâak kwàa ชอบมากกว่า

pregnant tháwng ท้อง

prepare, make ready triam เตรียม

prepared, ready triam phráwm เตรียมพร้อม

prescription bai sàng yaa ใบสั่งยา

present (here) thîi nîi ที่นี่

present (gift) khǎwng khwǎn ของขวัญ

present, to sanǒeh เสนอ

present moment, at the khanà níi ขณะนี้

presently, nowadays pàtcùban níi ปัจจุบันนี้

president prathaanaathíbàwdii ประธานาธิบดี

press, journalism kaan khàao การข่าว

press, to kòt กด

pressure khwaam kòt dan ความกดดัน

pretend, to klâehng แกล้ง

pretty (of places, things) sǔai สวย

pretty, cute nâa rák น่ารัก

pretty, very nâa rák mâak น่ารักมาก

prevent, to pâwng kan ป้องกัน

price raakhaa ราคา

pride sàksǐi ศักดิ์ศรี

priest phrá พระ

prime minister naayók rathamondrii นายกรัฐมนตรี

print, to phim พิมพ์

prison khúk คุก

private sùan tua ส่วนตัว

probably àat ca, pen pai dâi อาจจะ, เป็นไปได้

problem panhǎa ปัญหา

produce, to phalìt ผลิต

profession aachîip อาชีพ

profit phòn prayòht ผลประโยชน์

program, schedule kamnòt กำหนด

promise, to sǎnyaa สัญญา

pronounce, to àwk sǐang ออกเสียง

proof làkthǎan, khrûeang phísùut หลักฐาน, เครื่องพิสูจน์

property sǒmbàt สมบัติ

protest, to prathúang ประท้วง

Protestant lathí prohtaestâen ลัทธิโปรเตสแตนท์

proud phuumcai ภูมิใจ

prove, to phísùut พิสูจน์

public thîi sǎathaaraná ที่สาธารณะ

publish, to phim พิมพ์

pull, to dueng ดึง

pump sùup สูบ

punctual trong wehlaa ตรงเวลา

pupil nák rian นักเรียน

pure bawrísùt บริสุทธิ์

purple sǐi mûang สีม่วง
purpose cùt mûng mǎi จุดมุ่งหมาย
purse (for money) krapǎo ngoen
 กระเป๋าเงิน
push, to phlàk ผลัก
put off, delay lûean เลื่อน
put on (clothes) sài ใส่
put, place waang วาง
puzzled ngong งง
pyjamas sûea nawn เสื้อนอน

Q

qualification khunásǒmbàt คุณสมบัติ
quarter sèht nùeng sùan sìi
 เศษหนึ่งส่วนสี่
queen phrarâatchinii พระราชินี
question kham thǎam คำถาม
queue, line khiu คิว
queue, to line up khâo khiu เข้าคิว
quick reo เร็ว
quickly yàang reo อย่างเร็ว
quiet ngîap เงียบ
quite (fairly) phaw khuan พอควร
quite (very) mâak มาก

R

radio wítthayú วิทยุ
rail: by rail doi rótfai โดยรถไฟ
railroad, railway thaang rótfai
 ทางรถไฟ
rain fǒn ฝน
rain, to fǒn tòk ฝนตก
raise, lift yók ยก
raise, to (children) líang เลี้ยง
rambutan ngáw เงาะ
rank (military, police) yót ยศ
ranking kaan càt andàp
 การจัดอันดับ
rare (scarce) hǎa yâak หายาก
rare (uncooked) dìp ดิบ
rarely, seldom mâi khrâi ca...
 ไม่ใคร่จะ...

rat nǔu หนู
rate of exchange (for foreign
 currency) atraa lâehk plìan
 อัตราแลกเปลี่ยน
rate, tariff phaasǐi ภาษี
rather, fairly khâwn khâang ค่อนข้าง
rather than thaehn thîi ca...
 แทนที่จะ...
raw, uncooked, rare dìp ดิบ
reach, get to thǔeng ถึง
react to tàwp sanǎwng tàw...
 ตอบสนองต่อ...
reaction, response kaan tàwp
 sanǎwng การตอบสนอง
read, to àan อ่าน
ready phráwm พร้อม
ready, to get triam tua เตรียมตัว
ready, to make tham hâi phráwm
 ทำให้พร้อม
realize, be aware of rúu รู้
really (in fact) thîi cing ที่จริง
really (very) cing cing จริงๆ
really? cing lǒeh จริงหรือ
rear, tail khâng lǎng ข้างหลัง
reason hèht phǒn เหตุผล
reasonable (price) phaw
 sǒmkhuan พอสมควร
reasonable (sensible)
 sǒm hèht phǒn สมเหตุผล
recall, to núek àwk นึกออก
receipt bai sèt ใบเสร็จ
receive, to ráp รับ
recipe sùut aahǎan สูตรอาหาร
recognize, to cam dâi จำได้
recommend, to náenam แนะนำ
recovered, cured ráksǎa láeo
 รักษาแล้ว หายแล้ว
rectangle sìi lìam phúehn phâa
 สี่เหลี่ยมพื้นผ้า
red daehng แดง
reduce, to lót ลด
reduction kaan lót การลด
reflect, to satháwn สะท้อน
refrigerator tûu yen ตู้เย็น

R

refusal kaan patìsèht การปฏิเสธ

refuse, to patìsèht ปฏิเสธ

regarding kìao kàp เกี่ยวกับ

region phuumiphâak ภูมิภาค

register, to long thabian ลงทะเบียน

registered post còtmǎi long thabian จดหมายลงทะเบียน

regret, to sǐa cai เสียใจ

regrettably dûai khwaam sǐa cai ด้วยความเสียใจ

regular, normal pokkatì ปกติ

relatives (family) yâat ญาติ

relax, to phák phàwn พักผ่อน

release, to plàwi ปล่อย

religion sàatsanǎa ศาสนา

remainder, leftover thîi lǔea ที่เหลือ

remains (historical) sâak pràk hàk phang ซากปรักหักพัง

remember, to cam จำ

remind, to tuean เตือน

rent, to châo เช่า

rent out, to hâi châo ให้เช่า

repair, to sâwm ซ่อม

repeat, to tham sám ทำซ้ำ

replace, to thaehn แทน

reply, response tàwp ตอบ

reply, to (in deeds) tham tàwp ทำตอบ

reply, to (in speech) tàwp klàp ตอบกลับ

reply, to (in writing) khǐan tàwp เขียนตอบ

report rai-ngaan รายงาน

report, to rai-ngaan รายงาน

reporter phûu rai-ngaan ผู้รายงาน

request, to (formally) khǎw ráwng ขอร้อง

request, to (informally) khǎw ขอ

rescue, to chûai lǔea ช่วยเหลือ

research wícai วิจัย

research, to tham wícai ทำวิจัย

resemble mǔean เหมือน

reservation kaan cawng การจอง

reserve (for animals) thanǎwm ถนอม

reserve, to (ask for in advance) sǎmrawng สำรอง

resident, inhabitant phûu aasǎi ผู้อาศัย

resolve, to (a problem) kâeh panhǎa แก้ปัญหา

respect khwaam khaoróp ความเคารพ

respect, to nápthǔeh นับถือ

respond, react tàwp sanǎwng ตอบสนอง

response, reaction kaan tàwp sanǎwng การตอบสนอง

responsibility khwaam ráp phìt châwp ความรับผิดชอบ

responsible, to be ráp phìt châwp รับผิดชอบ

rest, remainder thîi lǔea ที่เหลือ

rest, to relax phák phàwn พักผ่อน

restaurant ráan aahǎan ร้านอาหาร

restrain, to dueng ao wái ดึงเอาไว้

restroom (for rest) hâwng phák ห้องพัก

restroom (bathroom) hâwng náam ห้องน้ำ

result phǒn ผล

resulting from, as a result pen phǒn maa càak... เป็นผลมาจาก...

retired plòt kasǐan ปลดเกษียณ

return home, to klàp bâan กลับบ้าน

return ticket tǔa pai klàp ตั๋วไปกลับ

return, give back hâi khuehn ให้คืน

return, go back klàp pai กลับไป

reveal, to (make visible) pòeht เปิด

reveal, to (make known) pòeht phòei เปิดเผย

reverse, to back up thǎwi lǎng ถอยหลัง

reversed, backwards klàp khâang กลับข้าง

ribbon ripbîn ริบบิ้น

rice (cooked) khâo sǔai ข้าวสวย

rice (uncooked grains)
 khâo săan ข้าวสาร
rice (plant) khâo ข้าว
rice fields naa นา
rich ruai รวย
rid: get rid of kamcàt กำจัด
ride (in car) nâng rót นั่งรถ
ride, to (animal) khìi ขี่
ride, to (transport) khûen ขึ้น
rights sìtthí สิทธิ
right, correct thùuk ถูก
right-hand side khwǎa ขวา
right now dǐao níi เดี๋ยวนี้
ring (jewelry) wǎehn แหวน
ring, to (on the telephone)
 mǔn thohrásàp หมุนโทรศัพท์
ring, to (bell) kòt kring กดกริ่ง
ripe sùk สุก
rise, ascend khûen ขึ้น
rise, increase phôehm khûen
 เพิ่มขึ้น
rival khûu khàeng คู่แข่ง
river mâe náam แม่น้ำ
road thanǒn ถนน
roast, grill yâang ย่าง
roasted, grilled, toasted pîng ปิ้ง
rock hǐn หิน
role bòt bàat บทบาท
roof lǎng khaa หลังคา
room (in house) hâwng ห้อง
room (in hotel) hâwng ห้อง
room, space thîi wâang ที่ว่าง
root (of plant) râak ราก
rope chûeak เชือก
rotten nâo เน่า
rough khrù khrà ขรุขระ
roughly, approximately pramaan
 ประมาณ
round (shape) klom กลม
round, around râwp râwp รอบๆ
rubber yaang ยาง
rude yàap khai หยาบคาย
rules kòt กฎ
run, to wîng วิ่ง

run away wîng nǐi วิ่งหนี

S

sacred sàksìt ศักดิ์สิทธิ์
sacrifice kaan sǐa salà การเสียสละ
sacrifice, to sǐa salà เสียสละ
sad sâo เศร้า
safe plàwtphai ปลอดภัย
sail, to lâwng ruea ล่องเรือ
salary ngoen duean เงินเดือน
sale, for khǎi ขาย
sale (reduced prices) lót raakhaa
 ลดราคา
sales assistant phanákngaan khǎi
 พนักงานขาย
salt kluea เกลือ
salty khem เค็ม
same mǔean เหมือน
sample tua yàang ตัวอย่าง
sand sai ทราย
sandals rawng tháo tàe รองเท้าแตะ
satisfied pen thîi phaw cai
 เป็นที่พอใจ
satisfy, to phaw cai พอใจ
Saturday wan sǎo วันเสาร์
sauce sáws ซอส
sauce (chili) nám cîm น้ำจิ้ม
save, keep kèp เก็บ
say, to phûut wâa พูดว่า
say hello thák thai ทักทาย
say goodbye bàwk laa บอกลา
say sorry bàwk sǐa cai บอกเสียใจ
say thankyou bàwk khàwp khun
 บอกขอบคุณ
scales taa châng ตาชั่ง
scarce mâi khâwi mii, hǎa yâak
 ไม่ค่อยมี, หายาก
scared nâa klua น่ากลัว
scenery, view wiu วิว
schedule kamnòt กำหนด
school rohngrian โรงเรียน
schoolchild dèk nákrian เด็กนักเรียน
science wíthayaasàat วิทยาศาสตร์

S

ENGLISH—THAI

scissors kankrai กรรไกร
Scotland sakàwtlaehn สก็อตแลนด์
Scottish, Scots chao sakàwt ชาวสก็อต
screen (of computer) caw phâap จอภาพ
scrub, to thǔu ถู
sculpt, to pân ปั้น
sculpture rûup pân รูปปั้น
sea thaleh ทะเล
seafood aahǎan thaleh อาหารทะเล
search for, to hǎa หา
season rúeduu ฤดู
seat thîi nâng ที่นั่ง
second thîi sǎwng ที่สอง
secret khwaam láp ความลับ
secret, to keep a ráksǎa khwaam láp รักษาความลับ
secretary lehkhǎanúkaan เลขานุการ
secure, safe mânkhong มั่นคง
see, to hěn เห็น
seed mét เมล็ด
seek, to hǎa หา
seem, to duu mǔean ดูเหมือน
see you later! phóp kan mài พบกันใหม่
seldom mâi khrâi ca... ไม่ใคร่จะ...
select, to lûeak เลือก
self ehng เอง
sell, to khǎi ขาย
send, to sòng ส่ง
sensible sǒm hèht phǒn สมเหตุผล
sentence prayòhk ประโยค
separate yâehk kan แยกกัน
separate, to càak kan จากกัน
September kanyaayon กันยายน
sequence, order taam lamdàp ตามลำดับ
serious (not funny) ao cing เอาจริง
serious (severe) rái raehng ร้ายแรง
servant khon chái คนใช้
serve, to ráp chái รับใช้
service bawríkaan บริการ
sesame oil námman ngaa น้ำมันงา

sesame seeds ngaa งา
set chút ชุด
seven cèt เจ็ด
seventeen sìp cèt สิบเจ็ด
seventy cèt sìp เจ็ดสิบ
several lǎi หลาย
severe run raehng รุนแรง
sew, to yép เย็บ
sex, gender phêht เพศ
sex, sexual activity rûam phêht ร่วมเพศ
shack krathâwm กระท่อม
shade rôm ngao ร่มเงา
shadow ngao เงา
shadow play lakhawn ngao ละครเงา
shake something, to khayào เขย่า
shake, to sàn สั่น
shall, will cà, ca จะ
shallow tûehn ตื้น
shame, disgrace lá-aai ละอาย
shame: what a shame! nâa khǎi nâa น่าขายหน้า
shampoo yaa sà phǒm ยาสระผม
shape rûup รูป
shape, to form tham hâi pen rûup ทำให้เป็นรูป
shark plaa chalǎam ปลาฉลาม
sharp khom คม
shave, to kohn โกน
she, her kháo เขา
sheep kàe แกะ
sheet (of paper) phàen kradàat แผ่นกระดาษ
sheet (for bed) phâa puu ผ้าปู
Shinto lathí chintoh ลัทธิชินโต
shiny pen ngao เป็นเงา
ship ruea เรือ
shirt sûea chóeht เสื้อเชิ้ต
shit khîi ขี้
shiver, to nǎo sàn หนาวสั่น
shoes rawng tháo รองเท้า
shoot, to ying ยิง
shop, store ráan ร้าน

shop, go shopping pai súeh
  kháwng ไปซื้อของ
shopkeeper khon fâo ráan, khon
  khǎi คนเฝ้าร้าน, คนขาย
short (concise) sân สั้น
short (not tall) tîa เตี้ย
shorts (short trousers)
  kaangkehng khǎa sân กางเกงขาสั้น
shorts (underpants) kaangkehng
  nai กางเกงใน
short time, a moment diao, mâi
  naan เดี๋ยว, ไม่นาน
shoulder bàa บ่า
shout, to takohn ตะโกน
show (broadcast) raikaan choh
  รายการโชว์
show (live performance) raikaan
  sòt รายการสด
show, to sadaehng แสดง
shower (for washing) àap náam
  fàk bua อาบน้ำฝักบัว
shower (of rain) fǒn ฝน
shower, to take a àap náam
  อาบน้ำ
shrimp, prawn kûng กุ้ง
shut pìt ปิด
shut, to pìt ปิด
sibling (older) phîi พี่
sibling (younger) náwng น้อง
sick, ill pùai ป่วย
sick, to be (vomit) ûak อ้วก
side khâang ข้าง
sightseeing pai thátsaná-cawn
  ไปทัศนาจร
sign, symbol sǎnyalák สัญลักษณ์
sign, to sen เซ็น
signature laisen ลายเซ็น
signboard kradaan prakàat
  กระดานประกาศ
silent ngîap เงียบ
silk mǎi ไหม
silver ngoen เงิน
similar khláai คล้าย
simple (easy) ngâi ง่าย

simple (uncomplicated, modest)
  thammadaa ธรรมดา
since tângtàeh ตั้งแต่
sing, to ráwng phlehng ร้องเพลง
Singapore sǐngkhápoh สิงคโปร์
single (not married) sòht โสด
single (only one) khon diao คนเดียว
sir (term of address) thân ท่าน
sister (older) phîi sǎo พี่สาว
sister (younger) náwng sǎo น้องสาว
sister-in-law (older) phîi saphái,
  phîi sǎamii พี่สะใภ้, พี่สามี
sister-in-law (younger)
  náwng saphái, náwng sǎamii
  น้องสะใภ้, น้องสามี
sit, to nâng นั่ง
sit down, to nâng long นั่งลง
situated, to be tâng yùu ตั้งอยู่
situation, how things are
  sathǎanakaan สถานการณ์
six hòk หก
sixteen sìp hòk สิบหก
sixty hòk sìp หกสิบ
size khanàat ขนาด
skewer mái sìap ไม้เสียบ
skilful mii tháksà มีทักษะ
skin phǐu ผิว
skirt kraprohng กระโปรง
sky fáa ฟ้า
sleep, to nawn làp นอนหลับ
sleepy ngûang ง่วง
slender sà-oht sà-ong สะโอดสะอง
slight lék náwi เล็กน้อย
slightly nít nàwi นิดหน่อย
slim phǎwm ผอม
slip (petticoat, underskirt) salìp
  สลิป
slippers rawng tháo tàe รองเท้าแตะ
slope lâat khǎo ลาดเขา
slow cháa ช้า
slowly cháa cháa ช้าๆ
small lék เล็ก
smart chalàat ฉลาด
smell, bad odor mii klìn มีกลิ่น

S

smell, to dom ดม
smile, to yím ยิ้ม
smoke khwaan ควัน
smoke, to (tobacco) sùup สูบ
smooth (to go smoothly)
 râap rîap ราบเรียบ
smooth (of surfaces) nian rîap
 เนียนเรียบ
smuggle, to lák lâwp ลักลอบ
snake nguu งู
sneeze caam จาม
sneeze, to caam จาม
snow himá หิมะ
snow, to himá tòk หิมะตก
snowpeas thùa wǎan ถั่วหวาน
so dang nán ดังนั้น
so, therefore dang nán ดังนั้น
soak, to chúp ชุบ
soap sabùu สบู่
soccer fút bawn ฟุตบอล
socket (electric) thîi sìap plák
 ที่เสียบปลั๊ก
socks thǔng tháo ถุงเท้า
sofa, couch sohfaa โซฟา
soft nûm นุ่ม
soft drink náam àt lom น้ำอัดลม
sold khǎi láeo ขายแล้ว
soldier thahǎan ทหาร
sold out khǎi mòt láeo
 ขายหมดแล้ว
sole, only khon diao คนเดียว
solid nâen แน่น
solve, to (a problem) kâeh panhǎa
 แก้ปัญหา
some bâang บ้าง
somebody, someone baang khon
 บางคน
something baang yàang บางอย่าง
sometimes baang thii บางที
somewhere sák hàeng สักแห่ง
son lûuk chai ลูกชาย
song phlehng เพลง
son-in-law lûuk khǒei ลูกเขย
soon nai mâi cháa ในไม่ช้า

sore, painful cèp เจ็บ
sorrow sâo เศร้า
sorry, to feel regretful sîa cai เสียใจ
sorry! khǎw thôht ขอโทษ
sort, type chanít ชนิด
sort out, deal with càt kaan จัดการ
so that phûea thîi ca... เพื่อที่จะ...
sound, noise sǐang เสียง
soup (clear) nám súp น้ำซุป
soup (spicy stew) tôm yam ต้มยำ
soup (chunky) súp kâwn ซุปก้อน
sour prîao เปรี้ยว
source sǎahèht สาเหตุ
south tâi ใต้
south-east tawan àwk chǐang tâi
 ตะวันออกเฉียงใต้
south-west tawan tòk chǐang tâi
 ตะวันตกเฉียงใต้
souvenir khǎwng thîi ralúek
 ของที่ระลึก
soy sauce (salty) sii-íu ซีอิ๊ว
soy sauce (sweet) sii-íu wǎan
 ซีอิ๊วหวาน
space thîi ที่
space (outer) awakàat อวกาศ
spacious thîi kwâang ที่กว้าง
speak, to phûut พูด
special phísèht พิเศษ
spectacles wâen taa แว่นตา
speech kham praasǎi คำปราศรัย
speech, to make a klào kham
 praasǎi กล่าวคำปราศรัย
speed khwaam reo ความเร็ว
spell, to sakòt สะกด
spend, to chái ใช้
spices khrûeang thêht เครื่องเทศ
spicy chùn, phèt ฉุน, เผ็ด
spinach phàk khǒm ผักโขม
spine kradùuk sǎn lǎng กระดูกสันหลัง
spiral kruai kliao กรวยเกลียว
spirits, hard liquor lâo เหล้า
spoiled (does not work)
 thùuk taam cai ถูกตามใจ
spoiled (of food) sîa เสีย

S

spoon cháwn ช้อน

sponge fawng náam ฟองน้ำ

sports kiilaa กีฬา

spotted (pattern) cùt cùt จุด ๆ

spouse khûu sǒmrót คู่สมรส

spray chìit sapreh ฉีดสเปรย์

spring (season) rúeduu bay mái phlì ฤดูใบไม้ผลิ

spring (of water) náam phú น้ำพุ

spring (metal part) sapring สปริง

spouse khûu sǒmrót คู่สมรส

square (shape) sìi lìam สี่เหลี่ยม

square, town square catùrát จัตุรัส

squid plaa mùek ปลาหมึก

staff câo nâa thîi เจ้าหน้าที่

stain rawi pûean รอยเปื้อน

stairs bandai บันได

stall (of vendor) ráan ร้าน

stall, to (car) yùt, kratùk หยุด, กระตุก

stamp (ink) thîi pám, traa pám ที่ปั๊ม, ตราปั๊ม

stamp (postage) sataehm แสตมป์

stand, to yuehn ยืน

stand up, to yuehn khûen ยืนขึ้น

star dao ดาว

start, beginning rôehm, tâng tôn เริ่ม, ตั้งต้น

start, to rôehm เริ่ม

stationery khrûeang khǐan เครื่องเขียน

statue rûup pân รูปปั้น

status, station in life thǎaná ฐานะ

stay, remain yùu kàp thîi อยู่กับที่

stay overnight, to kháang khuehn ค้างคืน

steal, to khamoi ขโมย

steam ai náam ไอน้ำ

steamed nûeng นึ่ง

steel lèk klâa เหล็กกล้า

steer, to hǎn phuangmaalai หันพวงมาลัย

step kâo ก้าว

steps, stairs bandai บันได

stick, pole mái sǎo ไม้เสา

stick out, to yûehn àwk maa ยื่นออกมา

stick to, to tìt kàp ติดกับ

sticky nǐao เหนียว

sticky rice khâo nǐao ข้าวเหนียว

stiff khǎeng แข็ง

still, quiet ngîap เงียบ

still, even now yang ยัง

stink, to měn เหม็น

stomach, belly sàdueh สะดือ

stone hǐn หิน

stool (feces) ùtcaaráa อุจจาระ

stop (bus, train) pâi, sathǎanii ป้าย, สถานี

stop, to halt yùt หยุด

stop, to cease lôehk เลิก

stop by, to pay a visit wáe แวะ

stop it! yùt ná หยุดนะ

store, shop ráan ร้าน

store, to sà-sǒm สะสม

storm phaayú พายุ

story (of a building) chán ชั้น

story (tale) rûeang เรื่อง

stout (plump) ûan, pûm pûi อ้วน, ปุ้มปุ้ย

stove, cooker tao เตา

straight (not crooked) trong ตรง

straight ahead trong pai khâng nâa ตรงไปข้างหน้า

strait châwng khâehp ช่องแคบ

strange plàehk แปลก

stranger plàehk nâa แปลกหน้า

street thanǒn ถนน

strength, power kamlang กำลัง

strict khrêng khrát เคร่งครัด

strike, to go on prathúang ประท้วง

strike, hit tii ตี

string chûeak เชือก

striped mii lai มีลาย

strong khǎeng raehng แข็งแรง

stubborn, determined dûeh ดื้อ

stuck, won't move tìt ติด

student nákrian นักเรียน

study, learn rian เรียน

stupid ngôh โง่
style bàehp แบบ
succeed, to sǎmrèt สำเร็จ
success khwaam sǎmrèt
ความสำเร็จ
such chên nán เช่นนั้น
such as, for example
tua yàang chên ตัวอย่างเช่น
suck, to dùut ดูด
suddenly than thii ทันที
suffer from, to thon thúk càak...
ทนทุกข์จาก...
suffer, to thon thúk ทนทุกข์
suffering kaan thon thúk การทนทุกข์
sugar námtaan น้ำตาล
sugarcane âwi อ้อย
suggest, to náenam แนะนำ
suggestion kham náenam คำแนะนำ
suit (clothes) sùut สูท
suitable, fitting, compatible
màwsǒm เหมาะสม
suitcase krapǎo sûea phâa
กระเป๋าเสื้อผ้า
summer nâa ráwn หน้าร้อน
summit, peak yâwt ยอด
sun phrá aathít พระอาทิตย์
Sunday wan aathít วันอาทิตย์
sunlight sǎehng aathít แสงอาทิตย์
sunny dàeht àwk แดดออก
sunrise phrá aathít khûen
พระอาทิตย์ขึ้น
sunset phrá aathít tòk
พระอาทิตย์ตก
supermarket súpôehmaakèt
ซูเปอร์มาเก็ต
suppose, to sǒmmút, khuan ca
สมมุติ ควรจะ
sure nâeh cai แน่ใจ
surf lên tôh khlûehn เล่นโต้คลื่น
surface phúehn phǐw พื้นผิว
surface mail praisanii thammadaa
ไปรษณีย์ธรรมดา
surname naam sakun นามสกุล
surprised plàehk cai แปลกใจ

surprising nâa plàehk cai น่าแปลกใจ
surroundings sìng wâeht láwm
สิ่งแวดล้อม
survive, to râwt chiiwít รอดชีวิต
suspect, to sǒngsǎi สงสัย
suspicion khwaam sǒngsǎi
ความสงสัย
swallow, to kluehn กลืน
sweat ngùea เหงื่อ
sweat, to ngùea àwk เหงื่อออก
sweep, to kwàat กวาด
sweet wǎan หวาน
sweet, dessert khǎwng wǎan
ของหวาน
sweet and sour prîao wǎan
เปรี้ยวหวาน
sweetcorn khâo phôht ข้าวโพด
sweets, candy khanǒm, lûuk om
ขนม, ลูกอม
swim, to wâi náam ว่ายน้ำ
swimming costume, swimsuit
chút wâi náam ชุดว่ายน้ำ
swimming pool sà wâi náam
สระว่ายน้ำ
swing, to kwàeng แกว่ง
switch sawít สวิทช์
switch on, turn on pòeht เปิด
switch, to change plìan เปลี่ยน
synthetic yai sǎngkhráw ใยสังเคราะห์

T

table tó โต๊ะ
tablecloth phâa puu tó ผ้าปูโต๊ะ
tablemat thîi rawng caan ที่รองจาน
tablets yaa mét ยาเม็ด
tail hǎang หาง
take, to ao เอา
take (away), to ao pai เอาไป
take out, to (remove) ao àwk
เอาออก
take care of, to duu laeh ดูแล
take off (clothes) thàwt ถอด
talk, to phûut พูด

talk about phûut rûeang พูดเรื่อง
tall sǔung สูง
tame chûeang เชื่อง
Taoism lathí tǎo ลัทธิเต๋า
tape record, to àt théhp อัดเทป
tape recorder khrûeang àt théhp
เครื่องอัดเทป
tape, adhesive théhp เทป
taste rót รส
taste, to (sample) chim ชิม
taste, to (salty) khem เค็ม
taste, to (spicy) phèt เผ็ด
tasty aràwi, mii rót châat อร่อย,
มีรสชาติ
taxi tháeksîi แท็กซี่
tea nám chaa น้ำชา
teach, to sǎwn สอน
teacher khruu ครู
team thiim, khaná ทีม, คณะ
tear, to rip chìik ฉีก
tears nám taa น้ำตา
teenager wai rûn วัยรุ่น
teeshirt sûea yûeht เสื้อยืด
teeth fan ฟัน
telephone thohrasàp โทรศัพท์
telephone box tûu thohrasàp
ตู้โทรศัพท์
telephone number mǎi lêhk
thohrasàp หมายเลขโทรศัพท์
television thii wii, thohrathát
ทีวี, โทรทัศน์
tell, to (a story) lâo เล่า
tell, to (let know) bàwk บอก
temperature unhàphuum อุณหภูมิ
temple (ancient) wát bohraan
วัดโบราณ
temple (Buddhist) wát วัด
temple (Balinese-Hindu) wát วัด
temple (Chinese) sǎan cáo
ศาลเจ้า
temple (Indian) surào สุเหร่า
temporary chûa khrao ชั่วคราว
ten sìp สิบ
tendon en เอ็น

tennis thennís, thennít เทนนิส
tens of, multiples of ten
lǎi sìp หลายสิบ
tense kreng เกร็ง
ten thousand mùehn หมื่น
terrible yâeh แย่
test trùat sàwp ตรวจสอบ
test, to thót lawng ทดลอง
testicles lûuk anthá ลูกอัณฑะ
Thai thai ไทย
Thailand mueang thai เมืองไทย
than kwàa กว่า
thank, to khàwp khun ขอบคุณ
thank you khàwp khun ขอบคุณ
that (introducing a quotation)
wâa... ว่า...
that, those nán, lào nán
นั้น, เหล่านั้น
that, which, the one who thîi ที่
theater (drama) rohng lákhawn
โรงละคร
their, theirs khǎwng kháo ของเขา
then láeo แล้ว
there thîi nân ที่นั่น
therefore dang nán ดังนั้น
there is, there are mii มี
they, them phûak kháo พวกเขา
thick (of liquids) khôn ข้น
thick (of things) nǎa หนา
thief khamoi ขโมย
thigh khǎa àwn ขาอ่อน
thin (of liquids) coeh caang เจือจาง
thin (of persons) phǎwm ผอม
thin (of things) baang บาง
thing khǎwng, sìng ของ, สิ่ง
think, to ponder trài trawng
ไตร่ตรอง
think, to have an opinion khít คิด
third (1/3) sèht nùeng sùan sǎam
เศษหนึ่งส่วนสาม
third... ...thîi sǎam ...ที่สาม
thirsty hǐu náam หิวน้ำ
thirteen sìp sǎam สิบสาม
thirty sǎam sìp สามสิบ

this, these níi, lào níi นี้, เหล่านี้
though máeh wâa แม้ว่า
thoughts khwaam khít ความคิด
thousand phan พัน
thread dâi ด้าย
threaten, to khùu ขู่
three săam สาม
throat khaw hăwi คอหอย
through, past phàan ผ่าน
throw, to khwâang ขว้าง
throw away, throw out
    khwâang thíng ขว้างทิ้ง
thunder fáa ráwng ฟ้าร้อง
Thursday wan pharúehàt
    (sabawdii) วันพฤหัสบดี
thus, so dang nán ดังนั้น
ticket (for transport) tŭa ตั๋ว
ticket (for entertainment) tŭa ตั๋ว
ticket (fine) bai sàng ใบสั่ง
tidy ñap ráwi เรียบร้อย
tidy up càt hâi dii khŭen
    จัดให้เรียบร้อย
tie, necktie nékthai เน็คไท
tie, to phùuk ผูก
tiger sŭea เสือ
tight nâen แน่น
time wehlaa เวลา
time: from time to time baangthii
    บางที
times (multiplying) khuun คูณ
timetable taaraang wehlaa
    ตารางเวลา
tiny lék náwi เล็กน้อย
tip (end) plai ปลาย
tip (gratuity) thíp ทิป
tired (sleepy) ngûang ง่วง
tired (worn out) nùeai เหนื่อย
title (of book, film) chûeh năng
    ชื่อหนัง
title (of person) kham nam nâa
    chûeh คำนำหน้าชื่อ
to, toward (a person) sùu สู่
to, toward (a place) pai yang ไปยัง
today wan níi วันนี้

toe plai tháo ปลายเท้า
tofu tâo hûu เต้าหู้
together dûai kan ด้วยกัน
toilet hâwng náam ห้องน้ำ
tomato makhŭea thêht มะเขือเทศ
tomorrow phrûng níi พรุ่งนี้
tongue lín ลิ้น
tonight khuehn níi คืนนี้
too (also) dûai ด้วย
too (excessive) koehn pai เกินไป
too much mâak koehn pai
    มากเกินไป
tool, utensil, instrument khrûeang
    mueh เครื่องมือ
tooth fan ฟัน
toothbrush praehng sĭi fan
    แปรงสีฟัน
toothpaste yaa sĭi fan ยาสีฟัน
top yâwt ยอด
topic hŭa khâw หัวข้อ
torch, flashlight fai chăi ไฟฉาย
total tháng mòt ทั้งหมด
touch, to tàe แตะ
tourist nák thâwng thîao นักท่องเที่ยว
toward pai sùu ไปสู่
towel phâa chét tua ผ้าเช็ดตัว
tower hăw khawi หอคอย
town mueang เมือง
toy khăwng lên ของเล่น
trade, business thurákìt ธุรกิจ
trade, to exchange lâehk plìan
    แลกเปลี่ยน
traditional dâng doehm ดั้งเดิม
traffic kaan caraacawn การจราจร
train rót fai รถไฟ
train station sathăanii rót fai
    สถานีรถไฟ
training kaan fùek การฝึก
translate, to plaeh แปล
travel, to doehn thaang เดินทาง
traveler nák doehn thaang
    นักเดินทาง
tray thàat ถาด
treat (something special) líang เลี้ยง

treat, to (behave towards) patìbàt tàw, tham tàw ปฏิบัติต่อ, ทำต่อ

treat, to (medically) ráksǎa รักษา

tree tôn mái ต้นไม้

triangle sǎam lìam สามเหลี่ยม

tribe chao khǎo, phào ชาวเขา, เผ่า

trip, journey kaan doehn thaang การเดินทาง

tripe phǎa khîi ñu ผ้าขี้ริ้ว

troops kawng tháp กองทัพ

trouble khwaam lambàak ความลำบาก

troublesome lambàak ลำบาก

trousers kaangkehng กางเกง

truck rót banthúk รถบรรทุก

true cing จริง

truly cing cing จริงๆ

trust, to wái cai ไว้ใจ

try, to phayaayaam พยายาม

try on (clothes) lawng sài ลองใส่

try out lawng ลอง

try out (food) chim ชิม

Tuesday wan angkhaan วันอังคาร

tuktuk taxi rót túk túk รถตุ๊กตุ๊ก

turn around, to líao klàp เลี้ยวกลับ

turn off, to pìt ปิด

turn on, to pòeht เปิด

turn, make a turn líao เลี้ยว

turtle (land) tào naa เต่านา

turtle (sea) tào tanù เต่าตนุ

TV thii wii ทีวี

twelve sìp sǎwng สิบสอง

twenty yîi sìp ยี่สิบ

two sǎwng สอง

type, sort chanít ชนิด

type, to phim พิมพ์

typhoon tâifùn ไต้ฝุ่น

typical pen thammadaa เป็นธรรมดา

U

ugly nâa klìat น่าเกลียด

umbrella rôm ร่ม

uncle lung ลุง

uncooked dìp ดิบ

under tâi ใต้

undergo, to tham ทำ

underpants kaangkehng nai กางเกงใน

undershirt sûea chán nai เสื้อชั้นใน

understand, to khâocai เข้าใจ

underwear chút chán nai ชุดชั้นใน

undressed, to get kâeh phâa แก้ผ้า

unfortunately chôhk rái โชคร้าย

unemployed wâang ngaan ว่างงาน

unhappy mây mii khwaam sùk ไม่มีความสุข

United Kingdom sahàràatchà-anaacàk, yuu kheh สหราชอาณาจักร, ยูเค

United States sahàrát amehríkaa สหรัฐอเมริกา

university mahǎawítthayaalai มหาวิทยาลัย

unless nâwk càak wâa นอกจากว่า

unlucky chôhk rái โชคร้าย

unnecessary mâi campen ไม่จำเป็น

unripe mâi sùk ไม่สุก

until con krathâng จนกระทั่ง

up, upward khûen ขึ้น

upset, unhappy kròht, mâi sabai cai โกรธ, ไม่สบายใจ

upside down ngǎi tháwng หงายท้อง

upstairs khâng bon ข้างบน

urban nai mueang ในเมือง

urge, to push for ñak ráwng เรียกร้อง

urgent rêng dùan เร่งด่วน

urinate, to chìi, pàtsawǎa ฉี่, ปัสสาวะ

use, to chái ใช้

used to, accustomed khún khoei, chin คุ้นเคย, ชิน

used to do something khoei เคย

useful mii prayòht มีประโยชน์

useless mây mii prayòht ไม่มีประโยชน์

usual pokkatì ปกติ

usually taam pokkatì ตามปกติ
uterus mót lûuk มดลูก

V

vacation wan yùt phák phàwn วันหยุดพักผ่อน
vaccination chìt wáksiin ฉีดวัคซีน
vagina cĭm, hĭi จิ๋ม, หี
vague khlum khruea คลุมเครือ
valid chái dâi ใช้ได้
valley hùp khǎo หุบเขา
value (cost) khâa, raakhaa ค่า, ราคา
value, good mii khun khâa มีคุณค่า
value, to tii khâa ตีค่า
vase caehkan แจกัน
VCR wii sii aa วีซีอาร์
vegetable phàk ผัก
vegetarian mangsawírát มังสวิรัติ
vegetarian, to be kin ceh กินเจ
vehicle rót รถ
very, extremely mâak มาก
vest, undershirt sûea yûeht เสื้อยืด
via phàan ผ่าน
video cassette théhp widiioh เทปวิดีโอ
video recorder khrûeang àt widiioh เครื่องอัดวิดีโอ
videotape, to àt widiioh อัดวิดีโอ
Vietnam wîatnaam เวียดนาม
Vietnamese chao wîatnaam ชาวเวียดนาม
view, panorama wiu วิว
view, look at chom wiu ชมวิว
village mùu bâan หมู่บ้าน
villager chao bâan ชาวบ้าน
vinegar nám sôm น้ำส้ม
visa wiisâa วีซ่า
visit yîam เยี่ยม
visit, to pay a pai yîam ไปเยี่ยม
voice sĭang เสียง
voicemail sĭang thaang mehl, wáwismehl เสียงทางเมล์ วอยซ์เมล์
volcano phuu khǎo fai ภูเขาไฟ

vomit, to aacian อาเจียร
vote, to wòht, long khanaehn sĭang โหวต, ลงคะแนนเสียง

W

wages khâa câang ค่าจ้าง
wait for, to raw รอ
waiter, waitress khon sòehp บริกร
wake up tùehn ตื่น
wake someone up plùk ปลุก
Wales wehl(s) เวลส์
walk, to doehn เดิน
walking distance doehn pai dâi เดินไปได้
wall kamphaehng กำแพง
wallet krapǎo sataang, krapǎo tang กระเป๋าสตางค์
want, to yàak อยาก
war sŏngkhraam สงคราม
war, to make tham sŏngkhraam ทำสงคราม
warm òp ùn อบอุ่น
warm, to ùn อุ่น
warmth khwaam òp ùn ความอบอุ่น
warn, to tuean เตือน
warning kham tuean คำเตือน
wash, to láang ล้าง
wash the dishes láang caan ล้างจาน
watch (wristwatch) naalíkaa นาฬิกา
watch, to (show, movie) duu ดู
watch, look, see mawng มอง
watch over, guard fâo เฝ้า
water náam น้ำ
water buffalo khwai ควาย
waterfall nám tòk น้ำตก
watermelon taehng moh แตงโม
wave (in sea) khlûehn คลื่น
wave, to bòhk mueh โบกมือ
wax khîi phûeng ขี้ผึ้ง

way, method wíthii วิธี
way: by way of doi โดย
way in thaang khâo ทางเข้า
way out thaang àwk ทางออก
we, us raw เรา
weak àwn aeh อ่อนแอ
wealthy mâng khâng มั่งคั่ง
weapon aawút อาวุธ
wear, to sài ใส่
weary nùeai เหนื่อย
weather aakàat อากาศ
weave, to thaw ทอ
weaving kaan thaw การทอ
website wép sáit เว็บไซต์
wedding ngaan tàeng ngaan
งานแต่งงาน
Wednesday wan phút วันพุธ
week sàpdaa, aathít สัปดาห์, อาทิตย์
weekend wan sùt sàpdaa
วันสุดสัปดาห์
weekly pracam sàpdaa ประจำสัปดาห์
weep, to ráwng hâi ร้องไห้
weigh, to châng ชั่ง
weight námnàk น้ำหนัก
weight, to gain námnàk khûen
น้ำหนักขึ้น
weight, to lose námnàk lót
น้ำหนักลด
welcome! yindii tâwn ráp ยินดีต้อนรับ
welcome, to tâwn ráp ต้อนรับ
well, good dii ดี
well (for water) bàw náam baadaan
บ่อน้ำบาดาล
well done! dii mâak ดีมาก
well-behaved tham tua dii ทำตัวดี
well-cooked, well-done sùk สุก
well-mannered maarayâat dii
มารยาทดี
well off, wealthy ruai รวย
Welsh chao wehl(s) ชาวเวลส์
west tawan tòk ตะวันตก
Westerner chao tawan tòk
ชาวตะวันตก
wet pìak เปียก

what? arai อะไร
what for? phûea arai เพื่ออะไร
what kind of? chanít nǎi,
bàehp nǎy ชนิดไหน แบบไหน
what time? kìi mohng láeo
กี่โมงแล้ว
wheel láw ล้อ
when? mûearài, mûearai เมื่อไหร่
when, at the time wehlaa เวลา
whenever mûearai kâw dai
เมื่อไรก็ได้
where? thîi nǎi ที่ไหน
where to? pai thîi nǎi ไปที่ไหน
which? nǎi ไหน
while, during rawàang, khanà thîi
ระหว่าง, ขณะที่
white khǎo ขาว
who? khrai ใคร
whole, all of tháng mòt ทั้งหมด
whole, to be complete sǒmbuun
สมบูรณ์
why? thammai ทำไม
wicked rái ร้าย
wide kwâang กว้าง
width khwaam kwâang ความกว้าง
widow mâeh mâi แม่ม่าย
widowed mâi ม่าย
widower phâw mâi พ่อม่าย
wife mia, phanrayaa เมีย, ภรรยา
wild (of animals) ...pàa ป่า
will, shall cà, ca จะ
win, to chaná ชนะ
wind, breeze lom ลม
window (in house) nâa tàang
หน้าต่าง
window (for paying, buying
tickets) khawtôeh, thîi khǎi tǔa
เคาน์เตอร์ ที่ขายตั๋ว
wine wai(n) ไวน์
wing pìik ปีก
winner phûu chaná ผู้ชนะ
winter nâa nǎo หน้าหนาว
wipe, to lóp ลบ
wire lûat ลวด

W

wise chalàat ฉลาด

wish, to praathanǎa ปรารถนา

with kàp กับ

with pleasure dûai khwaam yindii
ด้วยความยินดี

within reason phai nai khâw
camkàt ภายในข้อจำกัด

without pràatsacàak, doi mâi mii
ปราศจาก, โดยไม่มี

witness phayaan พยาน

witness, to hěn pen phayaan
เห็นเป็นพยาน

woman phûu yǐng ผู้หญิง

wonderful nâa pralàat cai
น่าประหลาดใจ

wood mái ไม้

wooden tham dûai mái ทำด้วยไม้

wool khǒn sàt ขนสัตว์

word kham คำ

work, occupation ngaan, aachîip
งาน, อาชีพ

work, to tham ngaan ทำงาน

work, to function tham ngaan ทำงาน

world lôhk โลก

worn out, tired nùeai, mòt raehng
เหนื่อย, หมดแรง

worn out (clothes) khàat mòt
ขาดหมด

worn out (machine) mòt aayú
หมดอายุ

worry, to klûm cai กลุ้มใจ

worse yâeh long แย่ลง

worship, to buuchaa บูชา

worst yâeh thîi sùt แย่ที่สุด

worth, to be mii khâa มีค่า

wound bàat phlǎeh บาดแผล

wrap, to hàw ห่อ

wrist khâw mueh ข้อมือ

write, to khǐan เขียน

writer nák khǐan นักเขียน

wrong (false) phìt ผิด

wrong (mistaken) khâocai phìt
เข้าใจผิด

wrong (morally) tham phìt ทำผิด

Y

yawn hǎo หาว

year pii ปี

years old pii ปี

yell, to takohn ตะโกน

yellow lǔeang เหลือง

yes châi ใช่

yesterday mûea waan níi เมื่อวานนี้

yet: not yet yang ยัง

you (intimate) thoeh เธอ

you khun คุณ

you're welcome! mâi pen rai
ไม่เป็นไร

young àwn อ่อน

younger brother or sister náwng
น้อง

youths (teenagers) nùm sǎo
หนุ่มสาว

youths (young people) yawachon
เยาวชน

Z

zero sǔun ศูนย์

zoo sǔan sàt สวนสัตว์

ENGLISH—THAI